Also by Sphere Books:

SOMETHING UNDER THE BED IS DROOLING
YUKON HO!
WEIRDOS FROM ANOTHER PLANET
LAZY SUNDAY BOOK

# Calvin and Hobbes®

by Bill Watterson

SPHERE BOOKS LIMITED

A Sphere Book

First published in the US by Andrews and McMeel 1987
Published by Sphere Books Ltd 1988
1st reprint 1989
2nd reprint 1990
3rd reprint 1990
4th reprint 1990



ISBN 0 7474 0288 4

Printed and bound in Great Britain by
BPCC Hazell Books
Aylesbury, Bucks, England
Member of BPCC Ltd.

Sphere Books Ltd
A Division of
Macdonald & Co (Publishers) Ltd
Orbit House
1 New Fetter Lane
London EC4A 1AR
A member of Maxwell Macmillan Pergamon Publishing Corporation

TO MELISSA

SO LONG, POP! I'M OFF TO CHECK MY TIGER TRAP!
I RIGGED A TUNA FISH SANDWICH YESTERDAY, SO I'M **SURE** TO HAVE A TIGER BY NOW!
THEY LIKE TUNA FISH, HUH?
TIGERS WILL DO **ANYTHING** FOR A TUNA FISH SANDWICH!
WE'RE KIND OF STUPID THAT WAY.
MUNCH MUNCH

SO DAD, WHAT DO I DO WHEN I CATCH A TIGER?
BRING IT HOME AND STUFF IT, CALVIN! CAN'T YOU SEE I'M BUSY?
SHEESH.
NO, REALLY, I COULDN'T EAT ANOTHER BITE!

WHAT'S ALL THIS NOISE? YOU'RE SUPPOSED TO BE ASLEEP!
IT WAS HOBBES, DAD! HE WAS JUMPING ON THE BED! HONEST!
"HOBBES" WAS ***NOT*** JUMPING ON THE BED! NOW GO TO SLEEP!
YOU WERE **TOO** JUMPING ON THE BED!
WELL, **YOU** WERE THE ONE PLAYING THE CYMBALS!!

SHOW AND TELL IS OVER, CALVIN. PLEASE PUT YOUR "TIGER" IN YOUR LOCKER.
IN MY LOCKER?! HE'LL SUFFOCATE!
WELL, AT LEAST PUT HIM UNDER YOUR CHAIR.
WHEW! THAT WAS A CLOSE ONE!
I'LL SAY!
SEVEN PLUS THREE.
SEVENTY-THREE.

GOOD NIGHT, CALVIN.
'NIGHT, DAD!
HEY! AREN'T YOU GOING TO SAY GOOD NIGHT TO HOBBES?!
GOOD NIGHT, HOBBES.
THAT'S IT ?! NO STORY? NO SMOOCH?!?
GO TO SLEEP, YOU SISSY.

WHAT'S THIS?
TASTE IT. YOU'LL LOVE IT.
YOU KNOW YOU'LL HATE SOMETHING WHEN THEY WON'T TELL YOU WHAT IT IS.

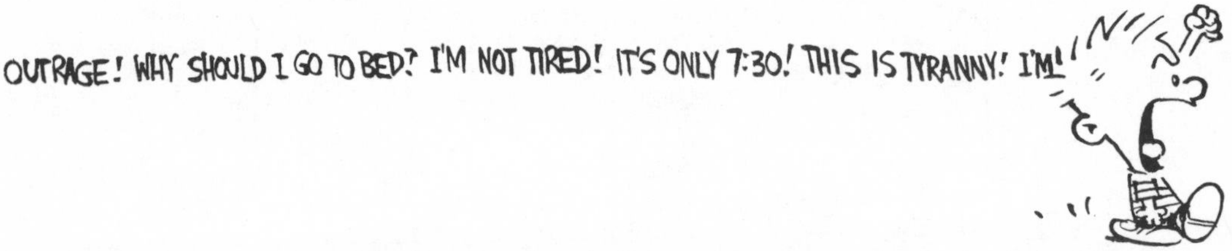
OUTRAGE! WHY SHOULD I GO TO BED? I'M NOT TIRED! IT'S ONLY 7:30! THIS IS TYRANNY! I'M!

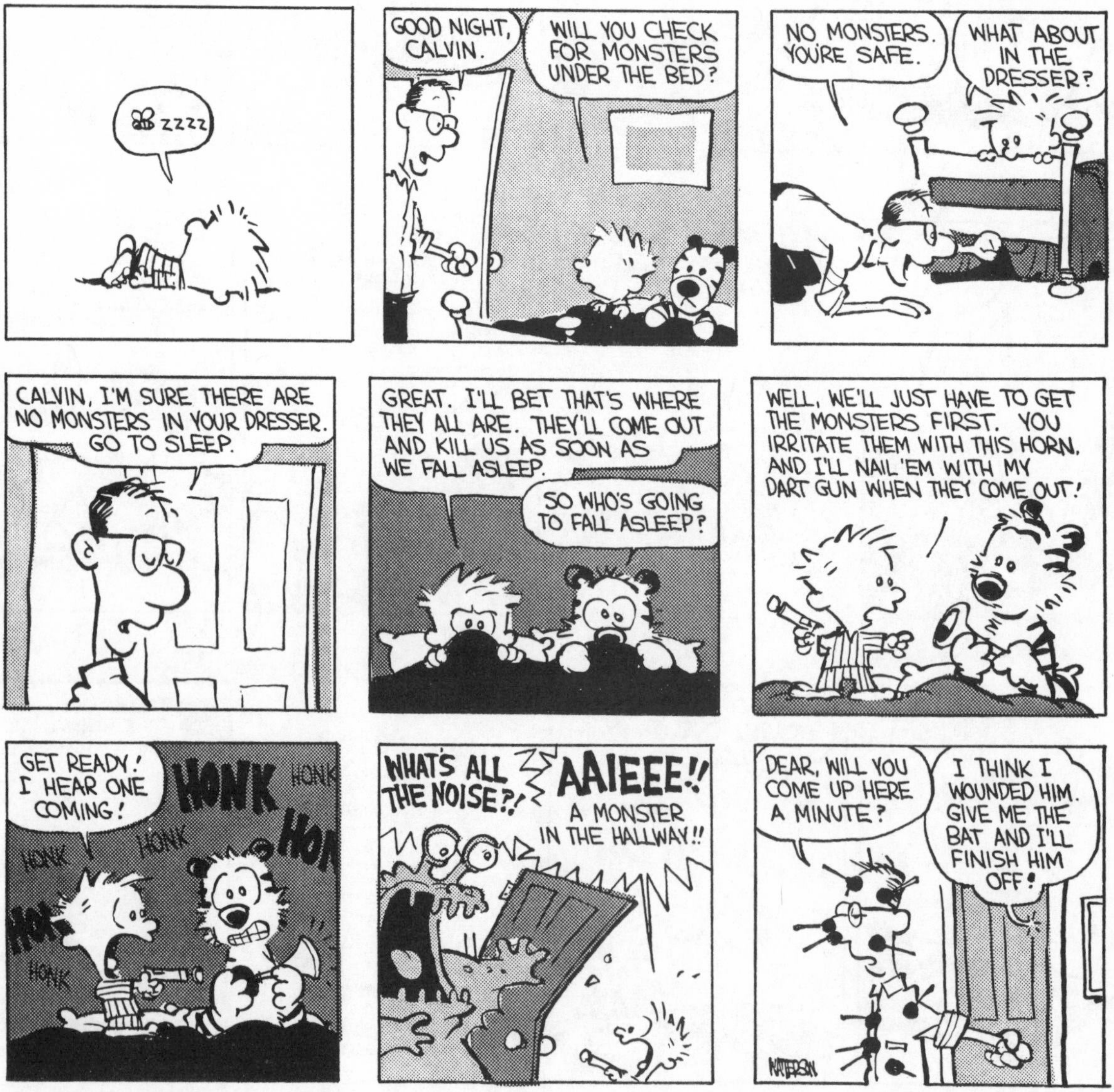
zzzz
GOOD NIGHT, CALVIN.
WILL YOU CHECK FOR MONSTERS UNDER THE BED?
NO MONSTERS. YOU'RE SAFE.
WHAT ABOUT IN THE DRESSER?
CALVIN, I'M SURE THERE ARE NO MONSTERS IN YOUR DRESSER. GO TO SLEEP.
GREAT. I'LL BET THAT'S WHERE THEY ALL ARE. THEY'LL COME OUT AND KILL US AS SOON AS WE FALL ASLEEP.
SO WHO'S GOING TO FALL ASLEEP?
WELL, WE'LL JUST HAVE TO GET THE MONSTERS FIRST. YOU IRRITATE THEM WITH THIS HORN, AND I'LL NAIL 'EM WITH MY DART GUN WHEN THEY COME OUT!
GET READY! I HEAR ONE COMING!
HONK
HONK
HONK
HONK
HONK
HON
HON
WHAT'S ALL THE NOISE?!
AAIEEE!! A MONSTER IN THE HALLWAY!!
DEAR, WILL YOU COME UP HERE A MINUTE?
I THINK I WOUNDED HIM. GIVE ME THE BAT AND I'LL FINISH HIM OFF!

ANY MONSTERS UNDER MY BED TONIGHT?!
NOPE!
NO!
UH-UH.
WELL, THERE'D BETTER **NOT** BE! I'D HATE TO HAVE TO **TORCH** ONE WITH MY FLAME THROWER!
YOU HAVE A FLAME THROWER??
THEY LIE. I LIE.

MOM, CAN I DRIVE ON THE WAY BACK?
OF COURSE NOT, CALVIN.
CAN I JUST STEER THEN? I PROMISE I WON'T CRASH.
NO, CALVIN.
CAN I WORK THE GAS AND BRAKES WHILE **YOU** STEER?
NO, CALVIN.
YOU NEVER LET ME DO ANYTHING.

HERE WE FIND A THRIVING CITY: BRAND NEW BUILDINGS, A BUSTLING ECONOMY.
A SCENIC THOROUGHFARE WINDS THROUGH THIS HAPPY MUNICIPALITY. HERE, A FARMER DRIVES HIS LIVESTOCK TO MARKET.
TRAGICALLY, THIS SERENE METROPOLIS LIES DIRECTLY BENEATH THE HOOVER DAM...

THIS SMELLS LIKE BAT BARF!
THAT DOES IT, YOUNG MAN! YOU ARE EXCUSED TO YOUR ROOM!
DON'T YOU THINK THAT'S A LITTLE HARSH, DEAR? HE'LL GET HUNGRY.
CALVIN HAS GOT TO LEARN SOME MANNERS! HE WON'T STARVE TO DEATH.
...AND EXTRA PEPPERONI!

WE'LL SEE WHAT THE PRINCIPAL HAS TO SAY ABOUT YOUR ATTENTION SPAN, YOUNG MAN!
THE VALIANT SPACEMAN SPIFF HAS BEEN CAPTURED!
THE ALIENS DOUBTLESSLY WANT THE SECRET FORMULA TO THE ATOMIC NAPALM NEUTRALIZER!
MOMENTS FROM THE TORTURE CHAMBER, SPIFF SPRINGS INTO **ACTION**!
WHY IS HE EATING HIS HALL PASS?

DO YOU BELIEVE IN FATE?
YOU MEAN, THAT OUR LIVES ARE PREDESTINED?
YEAH... THAT THE THINGS WE DO ARE INEVITABLE.
WHAT A SCARY THOUGHT!

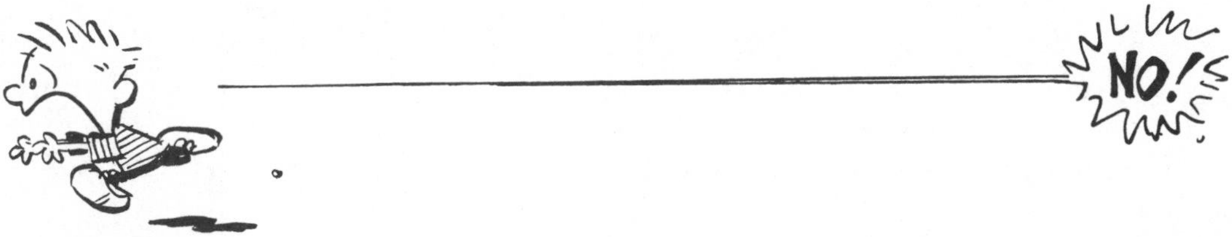
NO!

NO!
NO NO NO NO NO NO
GOODNESS, WHAT WAS ALL THAT FUSS?
OH, CALVIN DIDN'T WANT TO TAKE HIS BATH. WHAT A NOISY KID!
I'M DOOMED. I CAN'T BELIEVE MY OWN PARENTS WOULD DO THIS TO ME!
AH-HA! I'VE GOT YOU NOW, KID!
AAUGH! HELP! QUICK! MOMMM!
HA HA HA! HAVE A DRINK!
HELLP! GURGLE BLUB
CALVIN! QUIET DOWN AND QUIT THAT SPLASHING! I DON'T WANT TO HAVE TO CLEAN THE WHOLE BATHROOM!
WATTERSON
HA! I PULLED THE PLUG! DOWN THE DRAIN WITH YOU! DIE, FIEND! DIE, DIE!!
AAARRRGHHH
DON'T TELL ME HE'S LETTING THE WATER OUT ALREADY!
BELIEVE IT, LADY.

BAD NEWS, DAD. YOUR POLLS ARE WAY DOWN.
MY POLLS?
YOU RATE ESPECIALLY LOW AMONG TIGERS AND SIX-YEAR-OLD WHITE MALES.
IF YOU WANT TO STAY "DAD," I'D SUGGEST YOU ADOPT SOME KEY PLANKS TO YOUR PLATFORM.
WATTERSON
SOME SPECIAL INTEREST GROUPS ARE IN FOR A SURPRISE.
OF THOSE POLLED, VIRTUALLY ALL FAVOR INCREASED ALLOWANCES AND THE COMMENCEMENT OF DRIVING LESSONS.

THERE'S A NEW GIRL IN OUR CLASS.
WELL! WHAT'S HER NAME?
WHO KNOWS?
IS SHE NICE?
WHO CARES? NOT ME!
WATTERSON
DO YOU LIKE HER??
NO!

HERE COMES THAT NEW GIRL.
HEY SUSIE DERKINS, IS THAT YOUR FACE, OR IS A 'POSSUM STUCK IN YOUR COLLAR?
I HOPE YOU SUFFER A DEBILITATING BRAIN ANEURYSM, YOU FREAK!
WATTERSON
SHE'S CUTE, ISN'T SHE??
GO AWAY.

HI, CALVIN. MIND IF I JOIN YOU FOR LUNCH?
YES.
I HAVE SOUP TODAY. WHAT DO YOU HAVE?
A SQUID EYEBALL SANDWICH.
YOU DO NOT! DON'T BE DISGUSTING.
I LIKE TO SUCK OUT THE RETINAS.
MISS WORMWOOD!
CARE FOR A BITE? OR WERE YOU LEAVING?

YOU CAN'T COME UP HERE, SUSIE! NO GIRLS ALLOWED.
WHAT ON EARTH MAKES YOU THINK I'D WANT TO SIT IN A STUPID TREE IN THE FIRST PLACE ?!?
LEAVE IT TO A GIRL TO TAKE ALL THE FUN OUT OF SEX DISCRIMINATION.

WHEEEEEEEE
HOUSTON, WE HAVE A NEGATIVE ON THAT ORBIT TRAJECTORY.

OUR HERO, THE VALIANT SPACEMAN SPIFF, IS MAROONED ON A STRANGE WORLD...
I'LL SET MY MERTILIZER ON "DEEP FAT FRY."
CALVIN! YOU'RE NOT PAYING ATTENTION!
...WE JOIN SPACEMAN SPIFF ON THE DISTANT PLANET ZORG...
GRONK! ARGH!
ZOUNDS!
TRAPPED BY A HIDEOUS GRAKNIL, SPIFF DRAWS HIS TRUSTY ATOMIC NAPALM NEUTRALIZER!
CHEW ELECTRIC DEATH, SNARLING CUR!
BUT THE WEAPON IS USELESS! SPIFF IS DOOMED!!
OUR HERO MAKES A BREAK, AND DUCKS INTO A NEARBY CAVE!
WEEOOO! WHAT'S THAT AWFUL SMELL?
EEP!
TEACHERS LOUNGE
WHO WAS THAT?
BEATS ME, FRED.
SLAM!
WATTERSON

OH, MARY, YOU LOOK **RAVISHING** IN THAT SKIMPY NEGLIGEE!
KISS KISS
MMM...DARLING, DON'T YOU WISH WE WERE MARRIED?
BUT WE **ARE**! ...OR DID YOU MEAN TO EACH OTHER?
KISS KISS
I'VE GOT TO HAVE YOU! LET'S MURDER OUR SPOUSES!
**MURDER**?!--YOU SICK ANIMAL! I LOVE IT WHEN YOU TALK THAT WAY! COME HERE!
KISS KISS
SOMETIMES I THINK I LEARN MORE WHEN I STAY HOME FROM SCHOOL.
KISS KISS
WATERSON

MOM, CAN I SET FIRE TO MY BED MATTRESS?
NO, CALVIN.
CAN I RIDE MY TRICYCLE ON THE ROOF?
NO, CALVIN.
THEN CAN I HAVE A COOKIE?
NO, CALVIN.
SHE'S ON TO ME.
WATERSON

NO, MOM! DON'T PUT ME TO BED!
I INSTRUCTED HOBBES TO MESSILY DEVOUR ANYONE WHO BRINGS ME IN BEFORE 9 P.M.!
YOUR STUFFED TIGER IS IN THE WASHING MACHINE.
FINE TIME TO TAKE A **BATH**!
LISTEN, JUST BECAUSE **YOU** NEVER TAKE ONE...
PBTB!

DID YOU WATCH THE MOVIE ON TV LAST NIGHT?
NOPE.
DID YOU WATCH THE GAME THEN?
NOPE.
DID YOU WATCH **ANY** TV LAST NIGHT?
NOPE.
THEN WHAT DID YOU WATCH?

ZZZ...UNK.. GZ..YOW..ZZ..

Insurance 50¢
INSURANCE ?? WHAT A DUMB IDEA!
WHY WOULD ANYONE BUY INSURANCE FROM YOU ?!?
THWPING!
Insurance 50¢

BEEP BOOP
HELLO, DAD! IT IS NOW THREE IN THE MORNING. DO YOU KNOW WHERE I AM?

WE JOIN OUR HERO MEGAZORKS ABOVE PLANET GLOOB...
SPACEMAN SPIFF, CONQUEROR OF THE COSMOS, IS PURSUED BY THE HIDEOUS SCUM BEINGS OF PLANET Q-13!
SPIFF'S HYPER-FREEM DRIVE MALFUNCTIONS! THE ALIENS CLOSE IN!
SUDDENLY, A SEARING BOLT OF DEADLY FRAP RAY SLICES ACROSS THE BLACKNESS! OUR HERO IS UNFAZED.
ANOTHER BOLT! SPIFF IS HIT!!
PLOOIE!
SPIFF IS GOING DOWN! CAN HE MAKE IT?? IS THIS THE END?!!?
SPIFF'S ALIVE! HE MADE IT!!
AAAAAA
WATTERSON
I'M ALIVE! HA HA HA! I KISS THE SWEET GROUND!
MAYBE YOU SHOULD PLAY ON THE SWINGS, CALVIN.

CALVIN, ARE YOU GOING TO TAKE THAT STUFFED TIGER TO SCHOOL AGAIN?
SURE.
DON'T THE KIDS MAKE FUN OF YOU?
TOMMY CHESNUTT DID ONCE, AND NOW NOBODY DOES.
WHY, WHAT HAPPENED TO TOMMY CHESNUTT?
HOBBES ATE HIM!
UGH! HE NEEDED A BATH, TOO...

CALVIN! WHAT'S ALL THIS NOISE?! YOU'RE SUPPOSED TO BE ASLEEP!
MONSTERS UNDER THE BED, DAD! I WAS WHACKING ONE WITH MY BASEBALL BAT!
GOODNESS CALVIN, IT'S JUST YOUR STUFFED TIGER! YOU SHOULD PUT AWAY YOUR TOYS!
SORRY, OL' BUDDY. GOOD THING I MISSED OCCASIONALLY, HUH?
YEAH. LET ME SEE YOUR BAT A MINUTE.

HERE COMES THE SPORTS CAR AT 200 MILES PER HOUR!
HERE COMES A CEMENT TRUCK! LOOK OUT!
AND HERE COMES AN INFLAMMABLE CHEMICAL TRUCK! OH NO!!
THIS OUGHT TO BE GOOD.

DIG
DIG
PAT
PAT
CALVIN! WHAT ARE YOU DOING TO OUR YARD?!?
MAKING SPEED BUMPS.

I WONDER WHERE WE GO WHEN WE DIE.
PITTSBURGH?
YOU MEAN IF WE'RE GOOD OR IF WE'RE BAD?

WE'RE LOST AGAIN.
HA! WE'RE BRAVE EXPLORERS!
THE WORD "LOST" ISN'T EVEN IN OUR VOCABULARY!
HOW ABOUT THE WORD "MOMMY"?
MOMMMYYY!!

THERE! OUR FORTRESS IS COMPLETELY INDESTRUCTIBLE!
"SUNNY AND WARMER TODAY, HIGH IN THE UPPER THIRTIES..."
OUR SNOW FORT IS IMPENETRABLE!
AT THE SLIGHTEST PROVOCATION, WE'LL LET LOOSE A MERCILESS BARRAGE OF STINGING ICE!!
NONE DARE ATTACK US! WE RULE ALL!!
TOGETHER, A VERITABLE FIST OF DEFIANCE, WE STAND IMMUNE TO ANY ONSLAUGHT!
WE ARE INVINCIBLE!! WE...UH...UMM..
WATTERSON
PIFF!

HEY! WHERE'S THE STOCKING FOR HOBBES?
WHERE'S SANTA GONNA STICK HOBBES' LOOT, IF HOBBES DOESN'T HAVE A STOCKING?!?
OKAY, OKAY... I'LL MAKE HOBBES A STOCKING. DON'T WORRY.
MAKE IT BIG, BUT NOT AS BIG AS MINE.
..."HOBBES' LOOT"??
DON'T LOOK AT ME! I'M DONE SHOPPING!

ARE YOU STILL AWAKE?
OF COURSE!
IT'S MIDNIGHT. LET'S GO!
AS SOON AS HE DROPS THE BAG DOWN, YOU GRAB IT, AND I'LL CLOSE THE FLUE!

UH, HOBBES?... I FORGOT TO GET YOU A PRESENT. I DIDN'T EVEN MAKE YOU A CARD...
I'M SORRY, HOBBES. I DIDN'T MEAN TO FORGET.
IT'S OKAY, LITTLE BUDDY. I DIDN'T GET YOU ANYTHING EITHER.
BUT HERE'S A TIGER HUG FOR BEING MY BEST FRIEND.
NOT SO HARD, YOU BIG SISSY. YOU SQUEEZE MY TEARS OUT.
MERRY CHRISTMAS.

HOW LONG DO YOU THINK IT IS TILL BEDTIME?
OH, SIX OR SEVEN HOURS, I IMAGINE.
WHY DO YOU ASK?
WITH ANY LUCK, MOM WILL NOTICE WE'RE MISSING BY THEN.

WAP WAP WAP
CALVIN! WHAT ARE YOU DOING TO THE COFFEE TABLE?!?
IS THIS SOME SORT OF TRICK QUESTION, OR WHAT?

HEY CALVIN, YOU WANT TO PLAY "HOUSE"?
I DON'T KNOW. HOW DO YOU PLAY?
OKAY... FIRST, YOU COME HOME FROM WORK. THEN I COME HOME FROM WORK.
WE'LL GRIPE ABOUT OUR JOBS, AND THEN WE'LL ARGUE OVER WHOSE TURN IT IS TO MICROWAVE DINNER.

HNG
GAACKGURGLEPBTHFF
GRI
AGHPHHACKHACKPTU! PFTICKGPBHGRF
VERY GRIM, CALVIN. YOU'RE STILL HAVING OATMEAL.
GURGLE
QUIT PLAYING WITH YOUR OATMEAL AND EAT IT, CALVIN!
GAGPTH! I'M FREE! BLAUGH BLORK!
ICK
OOG
YAAH! DEATH TO OATMEAL!
KACHUNK!
AGH
BLOOP
ORG
YOU'LL NEVER ESCAPE, VILE GLOP! DIE! DIE!
IG
ORK
GOOK
CALVIN! QUIT...
..OH NO....
IT'S YOUR FAULT WE DIDN'T HAVE A SWEET LITTLE GIRL! YOUR STUPID CHROMOSOME!! NOT MINE!!
...I JUST LIVE HERE...
WATTERSON

IT SAYS HERE THAT BY THE AGE OF SIX ...
.. MOST CHILDREN HAVE SEEN A MILLION MURDERS ON TELEVISION.
I FIND THAT VERY DISTURBING!
IT MEANS I'VE BEEN WATCHING ALL THE WRONG CHANNELS.

I'M NOT EATING THIS GREEN STUFF. **YECCHH!**
GOOD IDEA, CALVIN. IT'S A PLATE OF TOXIC WASTE THAT WILL TURN YOU INTO A MUTANT IF YOU EAT IT.
!
RRGHHMPHFFG
MMMM
SCRAPE
URF
SMACK
GLUNK
URF
YUM
THERE HAS **GOT** TO BE A BETTER WAY TO MAKE HIM EAT!
AHHHH.. I CAN FEEL IT WORKING..

DAD, HOW COME YOU LIVE IN THIS HOUSE WITH MOM...
.. INSTEAD OF IN AN APARTMENT WITH SEVERAL SCANTILY CLAD FEMALE ROOMMATES?
BOY! ASK A SIMPLE QUESTION, AND GET ALL YOUR TELEVISION PRIVILEGES REVOKED.

HOBBES, HAVE YOU EVER KISSED A GIRL?
A FEW, I GUESS.
REALLY? WHAT WAS IT LIKE?
MMMMMMMMM
POP!
MFGHR!
...ONLY A LOT MORE SO!
GAACK! I WAS HOPING IT WOULDN'T BE SO FUZZY...

WHAT DO YOU FIND ATTRACTIVE IN WOMEN, HOBBES?
WELL, I'VE ALWAYS BEEN PARTIAL TO REDHEADS.
...WITH GREEN EYES. I LIKE GREEN EYES.
...AND WHISKERS! LONG WHISKERS!
LET'S CHANGE THE SUBJECT.

HAVING TRANSFORMED MYSELF INTO A WEREWOLF, I SEARCH FOR HUMAN SACRIFICE!
HI, DAD!
MM...HELLO.
CALVIN, STOP THAT DISGUSTING DROOLING!

I LOVE WINTER DAYS. THEY'RE SO PEACEFUL.
HA HA! GOTCHA, SUSIE!
WAP!
HEY, YOU DUMMY! YOU'LL NEVER BE ABLE TO THROW A SNOW BALL *THAT* BIG! HA! STUPID GIRL!
HEY, WHAT ARE YOU DOING? GET AWAY.
HEY! PUT ME DOWN! WHERE ARE YOU TAKING ME?! HEY! HEY!
CHUNK
WATTERSON

ALL RIGHT, CLASS, WHO WOULD LIKE TO GIVE HIS BOOK REPORT FIRST?
CALVIN, HOW ABOUT YOU?
CALVIN?
CALVIN?
SPACEMAN SPIFF COOLY DRAWS HIS DEATH RAY BLASTER...

2+7= ___
I cannot answer this qwestion, as it is against my religious principles.
IT'S WORTH A SHOT.

HOBBES, WHAT DO YOU THINK HAPPENS TO US WHEN WE DIE?
I THINK WE PLAY SAXOPHONE FOR AN ALL-GIRL CABARET IN NEW ORLEANS.
SO YOU BELIEVE IN HEAVEN?
CALL IT WHAT YOU LIKE.

WE ARE A FIERCE AND DIRTY BAND OF CUTTHROAT PIRATES!
KEEP A SHARP LOOKOUT, MATEY. WE WANT NO SISSY GIRLS ON OUR SHIP!
WE DON'T LIKE GIRLS?
OF COURSE NOT, DUMMY! WE'RE A MURDEROUS BUNCH OF PIRATES, REMEMBER?!
WHO DO WE SMOOCH THEN?

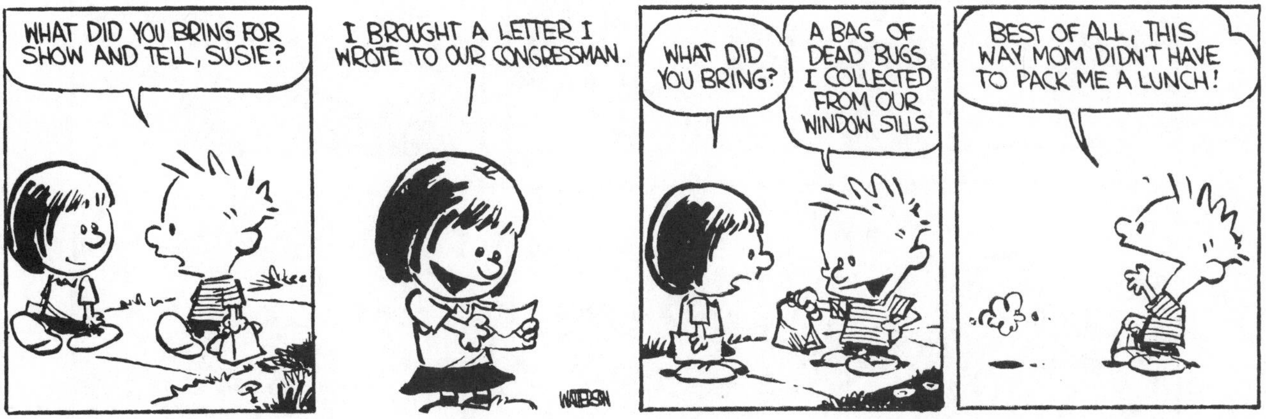
WHAT DID YOU BRING FOR SHOW AND TELL, SUSIE?
I BROUGHT A LETTER I WROTE TO OUR CONGRESSMAN.
WHAT DID YOU BRING?
A BAG OF DEAD BUGS I COLLECTED FROM OUR WINDOW SILLS.
BEST OF ALL, THIS WAY MOM DIDN'T HAVE TO PACK ME A LUNCH!

WELL, HOBBES, WE DID IT AGAIN. WE'RE SEPARATED FROM THE TROOP AND HOPELESSLY LOST.
FORTUNATELY, OUR MOTTO IS "BE PREPARED."
WITH THIS FULL BACKPACK, WE CAN STAY OUT HERE FOR WEEKS!
JUST SO LONG AS WE DON'T GET HUNGRY.
COMIX

I'M HOME FROM SCHOOL!
SO I GATHERED.
HOBBES?
YAAAAAH!
AAAAUGH! TIGER ATTACK!
GRRRR
RRRRRRRR
BINK BONK BANG BOING
CALVIN! QUIT CRASHING AROUND!
HOBBES JUMPED ME, MOM! I WAS FIGHTING FOR MY VERY SURVIVAL!!
SURE, CALVIN. LOOK, I DON'T WANT TO SEW HOBBES UP AGAIN, SO WHY DON'T YOU TWO GO DO SOMETHING QUIET?
OKAY, OKAY...
YOU SISSY. MOM ALWAYS TAKES **YOUR** SIDE!
THAT'S BECAUSE SHE WANTED ANOTHER TIGER, NOT YOU!
WATTERSON

CALVIN, PASS THIS NOTE TO JESSICA.
IT'S A **SECRET** NOTE, SO DON'T READ IT.
Calvin you stinkhead: I told you not to read this. Susie

THAT DIRTY SUSIE DERKINS. SHE'LL BE SORRY IF SHE TRIES TO PASS ANOTHER NOTE.
PSST...CALVIN! PASS THIS SECRET NOTE TO JESSICA, OKAY?
TEACHER! SUSIE'S PASSING NOTES!
TAKE THIS AWAY AND READ IT IN FRONT OF THE CLASS!
"DEAR JESSICA, YOU KNOW WHAT I HATE ABOUT CALVIN? HE'S A SQUEALER! SIGNED, SUSIE."
I HOPE YOU KNOW A GOOD DENTIST, SUSIE...

**NOW** LOOK! YOU GOT US SENT TO THE PRINCIPAL'S OFFICE!
GOSH! DO YOU THINK WE'LL GET PADDLED ??
THEY CAN'T PADDLE ME! I'M A GIRL!!
WHAT'S **THAT** GOT TO DO WITH IT?
GIRLS HAVE MORE DELICATE HEINIES.

CALVIN, I DON'T WANT TO BE SPANKED!
WHAT IF IT GOES ON OUR ACADEMIC TRANSCRIPTS? WE'LL BE RUINED!
* SNIFF *
WATTERSON
DARN YOU, CALVIN!! YOU'RE GONNA ANSWER TO MY PARENTS IF I CAN'T GET MY MASTER'S DEGREE!

CALVIN AND SUSIE, WOULD YOU COME IN MY OFFICE, PLEASE?
PRINCI
IT WAS ALL HIS FAULT, MR. SPITTLE!
THAT'S A LIE! SHE STARTED IT!
ARE YOU GOING TO SPANK US?!
I'LL NEVER PASS NOTES AGAIN! DON'T SPANK US!!
WATTERSON
WAAAHHHH!! I WISH WE WERE DEAD!!
I HATE THIS JOB.

NOW I WANT YOU BOTH TO PAY BETTER ATTENTION IN CLASS, UNDERSTOOD?
YES SIR.
OKAY, YOU MAY RETURN TO YOUR ROOM NOW.
THANK YOU, MR. SPITTLE.
WATTERSON
CALVIN? YOU MAY RETURN TO YOUR ROOM.
CALVIN?
THE ZORG DRAWS NEARER. SPIFF SETS HIS BLASTER ON "MEDIUM WELL"...

IT SAYS HERE THAT "RELIGION IS THE OPIATE OF THE MASSES." ...WHAT DO YOU SUPPOSE *THAT* MEANS?
..IT MEANS KARL MARX HADN'T SEEN ANYTHING YET..
WHAT ARE YOU WATCHING?
GARBAGE. THIS SHOW WOULD INSULT A 6-YEAR-OLD! AND I SHOULD KNOW.
SO WHY WATCH IT?
ALL THE OTHER SHOWS ARE EVEN WORSE!
WHY WATCH TV AT ALL THEN?
THERE'S NOTHING TO DO.
**NOTHING TO DO?!** YOU COULD READ A BOOK! OR WRITE A LETTER! OR TAKE A WALK!
WHEN YOU'RE OLD, YOU'LL WISH YOU HAD MORE THAN MEMORIES OF THIS TRIPE TO LOOK BACK ON.
UNDOUBTEDLY.
WATTERSON

..AND WITH THAT REPORT, WE...
CLICK
BEEEOOoooop
CLICK
RATS.

MOM, CAN I TAKE UP THE FLOORBOARDS IN MY ROOM AND MAKE A SECRET PASSAGEWAY?
OF COURSE NOT, CALVIN. DON'T BE RIDICULOUS.
WHY CAN'T I?
BECAUSE YOU'D COME RIGHT THROUGH THE KITCHEN CEILING. I SAID DON'T DO IT.
OKAY, OKAY...
HOW QUIETLY DO YOU THINK WE CAN NAIL THESE BACK IN?

WHAT'S THIS DISGUSTING SLIMY BLOB?
TRY IT. YOU'LL LOVE IT.
OH YEAH? WELL WHAT IF I DON'T LOVE IT?!?
THEN IT WILL BUILD CHARACTER.
THAT'S MY DAD. ALWAYS LOOKING OUT FOR ME.

CALVIN! YOU'RE GOING TO BE LATE FOR SCHOOL! GET UP!
CALVIN, IT'S ALMOST 7:30! ARE YOU UP??
I'M COMING.
SEE? I TOLD YOU IT WOULDN'T WORK!
OF COURSE NOT, DUMMY! YOU DIDN'T PUT ON ANY PANTS!

DO YOU KNOW WHERE BABIES COME FROM?
NOPE.
WELL, I WONDER HOW ONE FINDS OUT!
...HERE, LET ME SEE THE BACK OF YOUR SHIRT.
YOU CAME FROM TAIWAN.
WATTERSON

HEY, MOM, WHEN'S LUNCH?
LATER, CALVIN. I'M BUSY.
BUT I'M HUNGRY NOW! I WANNA EAT!
A MAP TO THE REFRIGERATOR. HILARIOUS.
WATTERSON

"McZARGALD'S ... NEXT EXIT... 50 MEGAZORKS."
"...OVER 75 MILLION EARTHLINGBURGERS SERVED..."
SPACEMAN SPIFF IS GOING DOWN!!!
WE JOIN OUR HERO AS HE STRUGGLES TO LAND HIS DAMAGED SPACECRAFT!
THE ALTITUDE FLAPS REFUSE TO RESPOND, BUT FEARLESS SPIFF IS UNFAZED!
SPIFF CAREENS THROUGH THE ALIEN CANYON! IS THIS *THE END*??
**NO!** MOMENTS BEFORE IMPACT, SPIFF EJECTS!
NOW ARE YOU THROUGH CHARGING AROUND THE HOUSE, OR ARE YOU GOING TO FALL DOWN THE STAIRS AGAIN?
OUR HERO REGAINS CONSCIOUSNESS AT THE FEET OF A SARCASTIC ALIEN...
WATERSON

HI, DAD. IT'S ME, CALVIN!
HOW'S WORK GOING? ...UH HUH... PRETTY DAY OUT, ISN'T IT? ... YEP.....
ARE YOU BRINGING ME HOME ANY PRESENTS TONIGHT? ... NO? WELL, JUST THOUGHT I'D ASK...
LISTEN, I SUPPOSE YOU'RE WONDERING WHY I CALLED...

DAD, YOUR POLLS TOOK A BIG DIVE THIS WEEK.
YOUR "OVERALL DAD PERFORMANCE" RATING WAS ESPECIALLY LOW.
SEE? RIGHT ABOUT YESTERDAY YOUR POPULARITY WENT DOWN THE TUBES.
CALVIN, YOU DIDN'T GET DESSERT YESTERDAY BECAUSE YOU FLOODED THE HOUSE!!
I'D SUGGEST A NEW LINE OF WORK, "DAD"...

THE GIANT SLIMY OCTOPUS OOZES ACROSS THE BEACH.
HIS HIDEOUS PRESENCE TERRORIZES THE SLEEPY WATERFRONT COMMUNITY.
WITH A SUCKER-COVERED TENTACLE, HE GRABS AN UNSUSPECTING TOURIST.
A MUFFLED SCREAM LINGERS IN THE SALTY AIR!
DID YOU WANT SOMETHING, CALVIN?
ACK
ICK
IG

UH-OH, HERE COMES MOE, THE CLASS BULLY!
Okay twinky, let's have that ball.
SURE, MOE. ALL YOURS
NEVER ARGUE WITH A SIX-YEAR-OLD WHO SHAVES.

Hey! You took my favorite swing!
THAT'S TRUE, MOE. HOW ABOUT THAT?
..uh..
HIS TRAIN OF THOUGHT IS STILL BOARDING AT THE STATION.

MOE, I WAS WONDERING SOMETHING.
ARE YOUR MALADJUSTED ANTISOCIAL TENDENCIES THE PRODUCT OF YOUR BERSERK PITUITARY GLAND?
what?
ISN'T HE GREAT, FOLKS? LET'S GIVE HIM A BIG HAND!

WHAT SHOULD WE HAVE DAD READ US TONIGHT?
..SO IN THE NEXT PANEL, SUPERTOAD GOES "PLOOIE," AND...
" 'MY, WHAT BIG TEETH YOU HAVE!' SAID LITTLE RED RIDING HOOD. 'THE BETTER TO EAT YOU WITH!' SAID THE WOLF..."
TIGER.
"...SAID THE TIGER, AND HE POUNCED ON LITTLE RED RIDING HOOD."
"JUST THEN A HUNTER CAME BY, AND WHEN HE SAW THE WOLF..."
TIGER.
"..WHEN HE SAW THE TIGER, HE PICKED UP HIS GUN AND..."
..AND?
"...AND IT WAS TOO LATE. THE TIGER ATE THEM BOTH AND HE LIVED HAPPILY EVER AFTER. THE END."
GOOD STORY, DAD! THANKS!
*SNIFF* I ALWAYS CRY AT HAPPY ENDINGS.
WATTERSON

"A BUSHEL IS A UNIT OF WEIGHT EQUAL TO FOUR PECKS."
WHAT'S A PECK?
A QUICK SMOOCH.
YOU KNOW, I DON'T UNDERSTAND MATH AT ALL.
WATTERSON

MOM, CAN I HAVE SOME MONEY SO HOBBES AND I CAN GO TO A MOVIE?
WATTERSON
WHAT MOVIE?
"THE CUISINART MURDERER OF CENTRAL HIGH."
I REALLY THINK THERE ARE MORE CONSTRUCTIVE WAYS YOU COULD SPEND YOUR AFTERNOON, CALVIN.
WHAT DID SHE SAY?
OH, SHE WENT OFF ON ONE OF HER IRRELEVANT TANGENTS AGAIN.

DO YOU BELIEVE OUR DESTINIES ARE CONTROLLED BY THE STARS?
NO, I THINK WE CAN DO WHATEVER WE WANT WITH OUR LIVES.
NOT TO HEAR MOM AND DAD TELL IT.
WATTERSON

READY?
NO.
♪
HURRY UP!
OKAY, I'M READY!
WATTERSON

I HAVE A QUESTION.
DO YOU BELIEVE IN LIFE AFTER DEATH?
YOU KNOW, REINCARNATION?
YOU JUST STEER, OKAY?
WATTERSON

MEEK AND MILD-MANNERED CALVIN DUCKS INTO A NEARBY CLOSET AND TRANSFORMS HIMSELF INTO...
CAPTAIN NAPALM
PROTECTOR OF THE AMERICAN WAY!
ENDOWED WITH SUPERHUMAN POWERS, HE QUICKLY...
MOMMMMMMMM!
WATTERSON

MAN THE HARPOONS! THAR SHE BLOWS!!
CAN HOBBES TAKE A BATH TOO?
NO, HOBBES DOESN'T NEED ONE. HOLD STILL.
BY GOLLY, WHAT IF I DROWN BECAUSE NOBODY WAS HERE TO RESCUE ME?!?
HOBBES! C'MERE!
MOM CAN'T KNOW YOU'RE IN HERE, OKAY?
I'LL DISGUISE MYSELF WITH BUBBLES.
HMM.. YOU NEED A HAT. HANG ON, AND I'LL GET ONE OF DAD'S.
I LIKE HIS GRAY ONE BEST.
MAYBE YOU SHOULD WEAR A TIE, TOO. I'LL BE RIGHT BACK.
BETTER HURRY! I THINK I HEAR YOUR MOM COMING!
DEAR! WHY ARE YOU TAKING A BATH?!? ... AND WEARING YOUR BEST HAT!!
WATERSON

WAKE UP, CALVIN. IT'S TIME FOR SCHOOL.
I'M NOT GOING TO SCHOOL ANYMORE.
YOU HAVE TO. IT'S THE LAW.
WHAT ABOUT HOBBES? WHY DOESN'T **HE** HAVE TO GO TO SCHOOL?
HE'S A TIGER. GET UP.
WHAT'S BEING A TIGER GOT TO DO WITH IT?
TIGERS WRECK THE GRADE CURVE.
WATTERSON

DO YOU THINK IT'S BETTER TO LIVE IN STUPEFYING SECURITY...
...OR TO TAKE RISKS AND LIVE LIFE ON THE EDGE?
*I* THINK IT'S BETTER TO ACCEPT DANGER AND LIVE TO THE FULLEST!
I TAKE IT BY YOUR SILENCE THAT YOU AGREE...
WATTERSON

I'M MAKING SUSIE DERKINS A VALENTINE.
SHE'S A CUTIE, ALL RIGHT.
SEE, I MADE A BIG RED HEART.
WATTERSON
NOW I'M PUTTING LACE AROUND IT.
THAT'S VERY SWEET. I'M SURE SHE'LL LIKE IT.
Susie, I hate you. Drop dead. Calvin

I'D LIKE TO GET A VALENTINE BOUQUET FOR A GIRL I KNOW.
WHAT A SWEET LITTLE BOY YOU ARE! COME SEE WHAT WE HAVE.
IS THIS ALL?
DID YOU HAVE SOMETHING SPECIAL IN MIND?
SORT OF. DO YOU HAVE A DUMPSTER OUT BACK I COULD ROOT THROUGH?

CALVIN, YOU BALONEY BRAIN!
!
YOU SENT ME A HATE-MAIL VALENTINE AND A CRUMMY BUNCH OF DEAD FLOWERS!
SO HERE'S A VALENTINE FOR **YOU**, YOU INSENSITIVE CLOD!!
POW
A VALENTINE AND FLOWERS! HE **LIKES** ME!
SHE NOTICED! SHE **LIKES** ME!

HEY, CALVIN! ARE WE NEAR A SLAUGHTERHOUSE, OR DID YOU FORGET YOUR DEODORANT?!
DROP DEAD, SUSIE! YOU'RE SO UGLY, I HEAR YOUR MOM PUTS A BAG OVER YOUR HEAD BEFORE SHE KISSES YOU GOODNIGHT!!

IT'S SHAMELESS THE WAY WE FLIRT.
WHAT'S IT LIKE TO FALL IN LOVE?
WELL... SAY THE OBJECT OF YOUR AFFECTION WALKS BY...
YEAH?
FIRST, YOUR HEART FALLS INTO YOUR STOMACH AND SPLASHES YOUR INNARDS.
ALL THE MOISTURE MAKES YOU SWEAT PROFUSELY.
THIS CONDENSATION SHORTS THE CIRCUITS TO YOUR BRAIN, AND YOU GET ALL WOOZY.
WHEN YOUR BRAIN BURNS OUT ALTOGETHER, YOUR MOUTH DISENGAGES AND YOU BABBLE LIKE A CRETIN UNTIL SHE LEAVES.
THAT'S LOVE?!?
MEDICALLY SPEAKING.
HECK, THAT HAPPENED TO ME ONCE, BUT I FIGURED IT WAS COOTIES!!
WATERSON

Hey, Calvin, it's gonna cost you 50 cents to be my friend today.
AND WHAT IF I DON'T *WANT* TO BE YOUR FRIEND TODAY?
Then the janitor scrapes you off the wall with a spatula.
HECK, WHAT'S A LITTLE EXTORTION AMONG FRIENDS?

I GOT THE NEW ALBUM BY SCRAMBLED DEBUTANTE.
ALL THEIR SONGS GLORIFY DEPRAVED VIOLENCE, MINDLESS SEX, AND THE DELIBERATE ABUSE OF DANGEROUS DRUGS.
YOUR MOM'S GOING TO GO INTO CONNIPTIONS WHEN SHE SEES *THIS* LYING AROUND.
WELL I SURE DIDN'T BUY IT FOR THE MUSIC..

MOM, WILL YOU DRIVE ME INTO TOWN?
WHY SHOULD I *DRIVE* YOU, CALVIN? IT'S A PERFECT DAY OUTSIDE!
WHAT DO YOU THINK PEOPLE HAVE *FEET* FOR?
TO WORK THE GAS PEDAL.

CALVIN, YOU'RE NOT PAYING ATTENTION AGAIN!
SPACEMAN SPIFF, CONQUEROR OF THE COSMOS, IS TRAPPED BY A HIDEOUS ZONDARG!
WITH LIGHTNING SPEED, SPIFF BOLTS FOR THE AIR LOCK, MAKING A DARING ESCAPE!
NICE TRY, CALVIN.

I'M HOME!
DID YOU FEED HOBBES TODAY, MOM?
NO, DEAR, IT MUST HAVE SLIPPED MY MIND.
THANKS, MOM. YOU WANNA JUST DOUSE ME IN STEAK SAUCE BEFORE I GO TO MY ROOM?

MOMMMM!
I'M THIRSTY!
WHAT'S THIS? JUST WATER?

HEY MOM, CAN I DRIVE NOW?
NO.
HOW ABOUT NOW?
KLUNK
OH NO!
OH YOU STUPID CAR! WHAT'S WRONG WITH YOU NOW?!?
THAT'S IT, MOM! GO AHEAD AND SWEAR! WE DON'T MIND!
CALVIN, BE QUIET!
WANT HOBBES AND ME TO GO GET HELP?
YOU STAY WHERE YOU ARE. I'LL LOOK UNDER THE HOOD.
KICK THE CAR, MOM! IT WORKS ON THE TV!
LOOK AT ALL THESE CARS GOING BY. NOBODY'S STOPPING TO HELP.
LET'S BLOW THE HORN! MAYBE SOMEONE WILL COME.
BEEEEP!
AAUGH!
BEEP! BEEP!
HOORAYY!! SOMEONE STOPPED! WE'RE HEROES!!
WANT ME TO CALL A TOW TRUCK, LADY?
FIRST CALL THE POLICE AND REPORT AN INFANTICIDE.
WATERSON

I NEED HELP ON MY HOMEWORK. WHAT'S A PRONOUN?
A NOUN THAT LOST ITS AMATEUR STATUS.
MAYBE I CAN GET A POINT FOR ORIGINALITY.
WATERSON

LEAVE YOUR TIGER IN THE CAR, CALVIN.
CAN'T HOBBES COME ALONG, DAD? HE WON'T EAT ANYBODY!
NO, CALVIN. LET'S GO.
WELL, AT LEAST LET ME OPEN THE WINDOW AND GIVE HIM SOME AIR.
SEE IF HE'LL LEAVE THE KEYS, TOO, SO I CAN LISTEN TO THE RADIO.
WATERSON

CALVIN, YOUR MOTHER AND I HAVE DECIDED TO GIVE YOU AN ALLOWANCE.
IT'S IMPORTANT THAT ONE LEARNS THE VALUE OF MONEY.
MONEY! HA HA HA! I'M RICH! I'M RICH! I CAN BUY OFF ANYONE! THE WORLD IS MINE!
WATERSON
POWER! FRIEND
PRESTIGE!
I BLEW IT AGAIN, DEAR!
I CAN BUY IT ALL! I'M FREE! HA HA HA HA!

WHEN I GROW UP, I WANT TO BE A RADICAL TERRORIST.
MM HMM..
I'M GOING TO INHALE THIS CAN OF PESTICIDE.
MM HMM..
I'M GOING TO WATCH TV ALL NIGHT.
THAT'S WHAT YOU THINK, BUSTER!
YOU CAN NEVER TELL IF THEY'RE LISTENING OR NOT.

HERE'S A GOOD MOVIE! "VAMPIRE SORORITY BABES"!
IT SAYS YOU HAVE TO BE EIGHTEEN TO GET IN.
HECK, THAT'S NO PROBLEM! LET'S GO!
THIS IS A NEW ONE.
TWO PLEASE. ...I MEAN, ONE.

I THINK IT'S TIME WE HAD A NEW DAD AROUND HERE. WHEN DOES YOUR TERM OF OFFICE EXPIRE?
SORRY, CALVIN, I WAS APPOINTED DAD FOR LIFE.
FOR LIFE?! WHAT ABOUT A RECALL VOTE? WHAT ABOUT IMPEACHMENT?
THERE ARE NO PROVISIONS FOR EITHER.
DID YOU WRITE THIS CONSTITUTION YOURSELF, OR WHAT?
WELL, YOUR MOM HELPED SOME, TOO.

ACHOO!
GESUNDHEIT!
OKAY! HOW MANY MONSTERS ARE UNDER MY BED TONIGHT?
JUST ONE.
THAT'S GOOD, HOBBES! WE OUTNUMBER HIM!
HEE HEE! WANNA GET HIM?
YEAH! SEE IF YOU CAN REACH THE BASEBALL BAT! HEH HEH!
QUIT SHOVING, YOU HOGS!
WATTERSON
MOMMMMM!
NICE GOING, MAURICE.

You're gonna taste asphalt fifth period, Twinky. Just so you know.
GREAT. I'M DEAD.
FIFTH PERIOD - "STUDIES IN CONTEMPORARY STATE-SPONSORED TERRORISM."
... ALSO KNOWN AS GYM CLASS.

I CAN'T GET A BABY SITTER ANYWHERE! WHAT SHOULD WE DO?
WE WON'T BE GONE LONG. COULDN'T CALVIN BE LEFT FOR A COUPLE HOURS UNSUPERVISED?
HA HA HA HA
HO HO HO HEE
HA
HOO
HAR
...SERIOUSLY... WHAT SHOULD WE DO?
HEE HEE

OKAY, CALVIN. WE'LL BE BACK IN A COUPLE OF HOURS.
YOU AND HOBBES JUST WATCH TV AND BE GOOD, OKAY?
DID YOU HEAR THAT? WE GET TO WATCH TV!!
HOORAY!
VIDEORAMA? I'D LIKE TO RENT A VCR AND SOME MOVIES!
ASK IF THEY HAVE "ATTACK OF THE COED CANNIBALS."

WELL, THE HOUSE IS STILL STANDING. CALVIN MUST HAVE GONE TO BED.
HIS LIGHT IS STILL ON. ... CALVIN? ARE YOU AWAKE?
EEP!
DID YOU WATCH A SCARY MOVIE ?!?
NO. DON'T COME IN. THE RUG IS RIGGED TOO.
WATTERSON

WHAP!
SMASH
TINKLE
DING
SHATTER
CLINK
WOW. FIRST TRY!
WATTERSON

WATTERSON
DOWNTOWN TOKYO!
AARRGHHGH
GODZILLA.

HOW CAN I GET SOME MONEY?
...SHORT OF EARNING IT, I MEAN...
I WANT A GRENADE LAUNCHER, MOM. WHEN'S CHRISTMAS?
NOT FOR A LONG TIME.
WHEN'S MY BIRTHDAY?
NOT FOR A LONG TIME.
WHEN'S MY ALLOWANCE?
YOU SPENT IT ALREADY.
DO I HAVE ANY STOCKS I CAN CASH? WAR BONDS??
CALVIN, I'M TRYING TO WORK!
CAN I BORROW SOME SOAP?
YES, YOU CAN BORROW SOME SOAP. HAVE ALL THE SOAP YOU WANT.
4 Sale CHEEP!
WATTERSON

BOY, IS IT COLD!
YOU SHOULD GET A GOOD FUR COAT LIKE MINE.
WATERSON
WOOF! WHAT DID YOU EAT FOR BREAKFAST? CEMENT?
LOOK, WAS THIS *MY* IDEA?

OH NO, I LOST MY QUARTER!
WHERE DID YOU LOSE IT?
IT'S SOMEWHERE IN THIS FIELD.
WE'LL NEVER FIND IT. YOU'LL HAVE TO WAIT TILL THE SNOW MELTS.
TILL THE SNOW MELTS? IT'S 25 CENTS!!
WATERSON
ZZZZZZZ

WANNA SEE SOMETHING WEIRD?
WATCH. YOU PUT BREAD IN THIS SLOT AND PUSH DOWN THIS LEVER...
THEN IN A FEW MINUTES, TOAST POPS UP!
DING!
WOW. WHERE DOES THE BREAD GO?
BEATS ME. ISN'T THAT WEIRD?

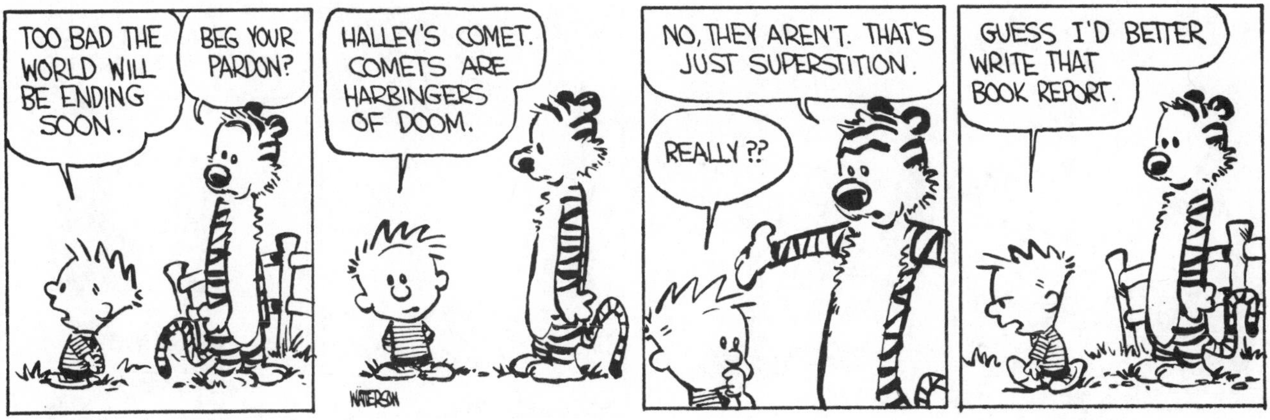
TOO BAD THE WORLD WILL BE ENDING SOON.
BEG YOUR PARDON?
HALLEY'S COMET. COMETS ARE HARBINGERS OF DOOM.
NO, THEY AREN'T. THAT'S JUST SUPERSTITION.
REALLY ??
GUESS I'D BETTER WRITE THAT BOOK REPORT.

HOW ARE YOU TODAY?
FINE.
I WANT THE TOP OF MY HEAD SHAVED, AND THE SIDES DYED PINK AND CUT IN HORIZONTAL STRIPES, OK?
MA'AM?
GIVE HIM THE USUAL, PETE.
WATTERSON
WELL I GUESS THIS GUY KNOWS WHICH SIDE **HIS** BREAD IS BUTTERED ON!

THERE, HOW'S THAT LOOK?
THAT'S GREAT. PERFECT.
WITHOUT QUESTION, THIS IS THE FINEST HAIRCUT I HAVE EVER RECEIVED.
NEVER CRITICIZE A GUY WITH A RAZOR...
WATTERSON

PIZZA

READY?
LET ME CHECK WHAT THE DEDUCTIBLE IS ON MY INSURANCE POLICY...
MUNCH MUNCH
WOULD YOU CARE FOR A SOFT DRINK?
OK.
H-H-HERE Y-YOU A-A-ARE!
BONK!
BONK!
ANY DESSERT?
NO, THANKS.
WE'LL BE LANDING SHORTLY.
THE CAPTAIN HAS TURNED OFF THE SEAT BELT SIGN. THANK YOU FOR CHOOSING CALVIN'S FLIGHT 240 NON-STOP TO STONEY GULCH.
NEXT TIME I WON'T TAKE THE DINNER FLIGHT.
WATTERSON

DO YOU LOVE ME, DAD?
OF COURSE I DO, CALVIN.
WOULD YOU STILL LOVE ME IF I DID SOMETHING BAD?
WELL OF COURSE ... I ... WOULD...
I MEAN SOMETHING REALLY *REALLY*..
CALVIN, WHAT DID YOU DO?!

WELL, DAD, YOUR POLLS ARE REAL HIGH THIS WEEK.
I'M GLAD TO HEAR THAT.
YEP, THOSE POLLED THINK YOU'RE DOING A FINE JOB AS DAD.
IN FACT, WITH A LITTLE PUSH TODAY, YOUR POLITICAL STOCK COULD REACH A RECORD HIGH.
NICE TRY. GO HELP YOUR MOM WITH THE DISHES.
OOH DAD! SUICIDE! OOH! OOH!

HERE COMES MOE, THE CLASS BULLY.
HE'S NOT SMART, BUT HE'S STREETWISE.
THAT MEANS HE KNOWS WHAT STREET HE LIVES ON.

TOLL BOOTH, DAD! YOU CAN'T PUT THE CAR IN UNTIL YOU PAY ME A QUARTER!
WHY SHOULD I PAY YOU TO PUT *MY* CAR IN *MY* GARAGE?
BECAUSE IF YOU DON'T, I'LL PULL THE DOOR DOWN ON THE HOOD AS YOU DRIVE IN!
WHAT A CHEAPSKATE.

A LITTLE LOWER...OK, FINE!
THANKS FOR HELPING ME PUT UP THIS SWING.
WHERE DID YOU EVER FIND THIS GREAT TIRE?
CALVIN! I'VE GOT TO GO TO WORK!!

WHAT'S THAT CEREAL YOU'RE EATING?
IT'S MY NEW FAVORITE, "CHOCOLATE FROSTED SUGAR BOMBS."
HAVE A TASTE.
THANK YOU.
MFFPBTH!! S-SW-SW SWEET!!
ACTUALLY, THEY'RE KINDA BLAND TILL YOU SCOOP SUGAR ON 'EM.

HOW COME WE PLAY WAR AND NOT PEACE?
TOO FEW ROLE MODELS.
I'LL BE THE FEARLESS AMERICAN DEFENDER OF LIBERTY AND DEMOCRACY..
...AND YOU CAN BE THE LOATHSOME GODLESS COMMUNIST OPPRESSOR.
WE'RE AT WAR, SO IF YOU GET HIT WITH A DART, YOU'RE DEAD AND THE OTHER SIDE WINS, OK?
GOTCHA.
GO!
WAP
WAP
KIND OF A STUPID GAME, ISN'T IT?
WATTERSON

CAN I BE EXCUSED?
NOT UNTIL YOU FINISH YOUR SALMON.
BLAUGHHH!
CAN I EAT IT UPSTAIRS WHILE I DO MY HOMEWORK?
WELL, I SUPPOSE.
I BROUGHT YOU YOUR FAVORITE! HOW'S IT COMING?
WELL, I COULDN'T FIGURE OUT THIS SUBTRACTION PROBLEM, SO I PUT "ATLANTA, GEORGIA"...
WATTERSON

HEY, SUSIE, WANNA SEE A MAGIC TRICK?
FIRST, I'LL NEED AN ORDINARY QUARTER...
!
NOW I'LL DISAPPEAR! HA HA HA!
HEY! DIDN'T I SAY IT WAS A TRICK??
WATTERSON

LOOK! A DECODER RING!
WOW! WE CAN SEND EACH OTHER SECRET MESSAGES IN CODE!
HA HA! NOW MOM AND DAD WON'T BE ABLE TO UNDERSTAND US AT ALL!
...NOT THAT THEY DO ANYWAY...
WATTERSON

RISE AND SHINE, CALVIN!
MFGPBTHBBPT
THE EARLY BIRD GETS THE WORM!
BIG INCENTIVE.

I'VE DECIDED WE SHOULD BE "COOLER" THAN WE ARE.
WE'RE NOT COOL?
SURE WE'RE COOL. BUT WE'RE NOT AS COOL AS WE COULD BE.
COOL PEOPLE WEAR DARK GLASSES!
IT'S COOL TO BUMP INTO THINGS?
YOU DON'T MOVE, YOU JUST HANG AROUND.

HEY, DAD, WILL YOU BUY ME A FLAME THROWER?
OF COURSE NOT. DON'T BE SILLY.
EVEN IF I DIDN'T USE IT IN THE HOUSE?

DID YOU ASK YOUR MOM IF YOU COULD JUMP OFF THE ROOF?
QUESTIONS I KNOW THE ANSWERS TO I DON'T NEED TO ASK, RIGHT?
IS THIS BLANKET BIG ENOUGH?
PERFECT!
SEE, I'LL JUST GRAB ALL THE CORNERS AND MAKE A PARACHUTE!
YOU CAN WATCH AS I FLOAT TO THE GROUND, GENTLY AS A LEAF!
GERONIMO!!
CRUNCH
HIS MOM'S GOING TO HAVE A FIT ABOUT THOSE ROSE BUSHES.
WATTERSON

I TOLD YOU I'M NOT SICK! WHAT'S THAT? WILL IT HURT?
IT'S A TONGUE DEPRESSOR. IT WON'T HURT AT ALL.
WHAT'S THAT? WILL IT HURT?
IT'S A STETHOSCOPE. IT WON'T HURT AT ALL.
WHAT'S THAT? WILL IT HURT?
IT'S A CATTLE PROD. IT HURTS A LITTLE LESS THAN A BRANDING IRON.
LITTLE KIDS HAVE NO SENSE OF HUMOR.

HEY, DOC, WHY ARE YOU RUBBING MY ARM WITH COTTON? ARE YOU GOING TO PUT A LEECH THERE?
ARE YOU GOING TO BLEED ME? YOU'RE NOT GOING TO AMPUTATE, ARE YOU? ARE YOU??
WHAT'S THAT? IS THAT A SHOT? ARE YOU GOING TO... AAUGHH! IT WENT CLEAR THROUGH MY ARM!! OW OW OW OW!!!
I'M DYING! I HOPE YOU'VE PAID YOUR MALPRACTICE INSURANCE, YOU QUACK!! WHERE'S MY MOM??!

"SAFARI AL" HACKS HIS WAY THROUGH THE JUNGLE!
SUDDENLY, A GIANT GORILLA RIPS THROUGH THE FOLIAGE!
CLEAN YOUR ROOM.
WHAT?
YOU HEARD ME. IT'S A JUNGLE IN HERE!

SEEN ANY UFOs YET?
NOPE.
KEEP WATCHING THE MOON. ALIENS USUALLY TRY TO SNEAK UP FROM BEHIND IT.
WHAT ARE YOU DOING OUT HERE IN YOUR PAJAMAS? GET BACK IN BED!!
MOTHERS, ON THE OTHER HAND, SNEAK UP FROM BEHIND THE PACHYSANDRA PATCH.

I DON'T THINK I'LL GO TO SCHOOL TODAY.
I THINK YOU WILL.
I THINK I WON'T.
RATS.
WATTERSON

GOOD NIGHT, HOBBES.
GOOD NIGHT.
DO YOU BELIEVE IN GHOSTS?
WATTERSON

WHAT DO YOU HAVE FOR LUNCH, SUSIE? MAYBE I'LL TRADE YOU.
IT'S BOLOGNA!
UGH! A CROSS SECTION OF A DACHSHUND. NO, THANKS.
I WONDER WHAT I HAVE FOR LUNCH TODAY.
IT'S LUNCH TIME! HA HA HA! I THINK I'LL HAVE THIS LITTLE KID!!
HELP! I'M BEING EATEN ALIVE BY MY OWN LUNCH! SOMEBODY GET ME A FORK!
HE'S GOT ME!!
AAARRRGGHH
WHAM
WHAM
WHAM
WHAM
HA! I KILLED IT WITH MY THERMOS! SEE? IT'S BLEEDING JELLY!
NO WONDER THIS SEAT WASN'T TAKEN.
WATTERSON

SOMEWHERE IN COMMUNIST RUSSIA I'LL BET THERE'S A LITTLE BOY WHO HAS NEVER KNOWN ANYTHING BUT **CENSORSHIP** AND **OPPRESSION**.
BUT MAYBE HE'S HEARD ABOUT **AMERICA**, AND HE DREAMS OF LIVING IN THIS LAND OF **FREEDOM** AND OPPORTUNITY!
SOMEDAY, I'D LIKE TO MEET THAT LITTLE BOY...
...AND TELL HIM THE AWFUL **TRUTH** ABOUT THIS PLACE!!
CALVIN, BE QUIET AND EAT THE STUPID LIMA BEANS.

WHENEVER I TAKE MY BATH...
...I ALWAYS PUT MY DUCKY IN FIRST.
FOR COMPANIONSHIP?
TO TEST FOR SHARKS.

MY SECRET ANCIENT TREASURE MAP SAYS TO DIG HERE!
LOOK! A WALLET FULL OF MONEY! RIGHT WHERE YOU SAID!
IT'S DAD'S. I BURIED IT HERE LAST WEEK.

SPACEMAN SPIFF, BOLD INTERPLANETARY EXPLORER, SPIES A ZARG!
SPIFF CALIBRATES HIS BLASTER. READY...AIM...
CALVIN, IF YOU SHOOT THAT PAPER CLIP AT ME, I'LL GET YOUR BOTTOM HAULED TO THE PRINCIPAL'S OFFICE SO FAST YOU'LL THINK YOU WERE IN A **TIME WARP**!!
CONFOUND IT. THE BLASTER JAMMED.

IT LOOKS LIKE HOBBES BURST A SEAM HERE. I'LL GET MY SEWING KIT.
IT'S JUST A LITTLE CUT. I DON'T NEED AN OPERATION. THIS IS UNNECESSARY SURGERY!
IT'S NOT SURGERY. YOU'RE JUST GETTING A COUPLE STITCHES! WHAT'S THE BIG DEAL?
YOUR MOM NEVER USES ANY ANESTHETIC.

WHAT A PECULIAR DREAM I HAD LAST NIGHT!
I DREAMED I WAS IN A BIG FIGHT WITH A FEROCIOUS WEASEL!
WHAT DO YOU SUPPOSE IT MEANS?
IT MEANS YOU'RE SLEEPING ON THE FLOOR TONIGHT, YOU NINCOMPOOP!

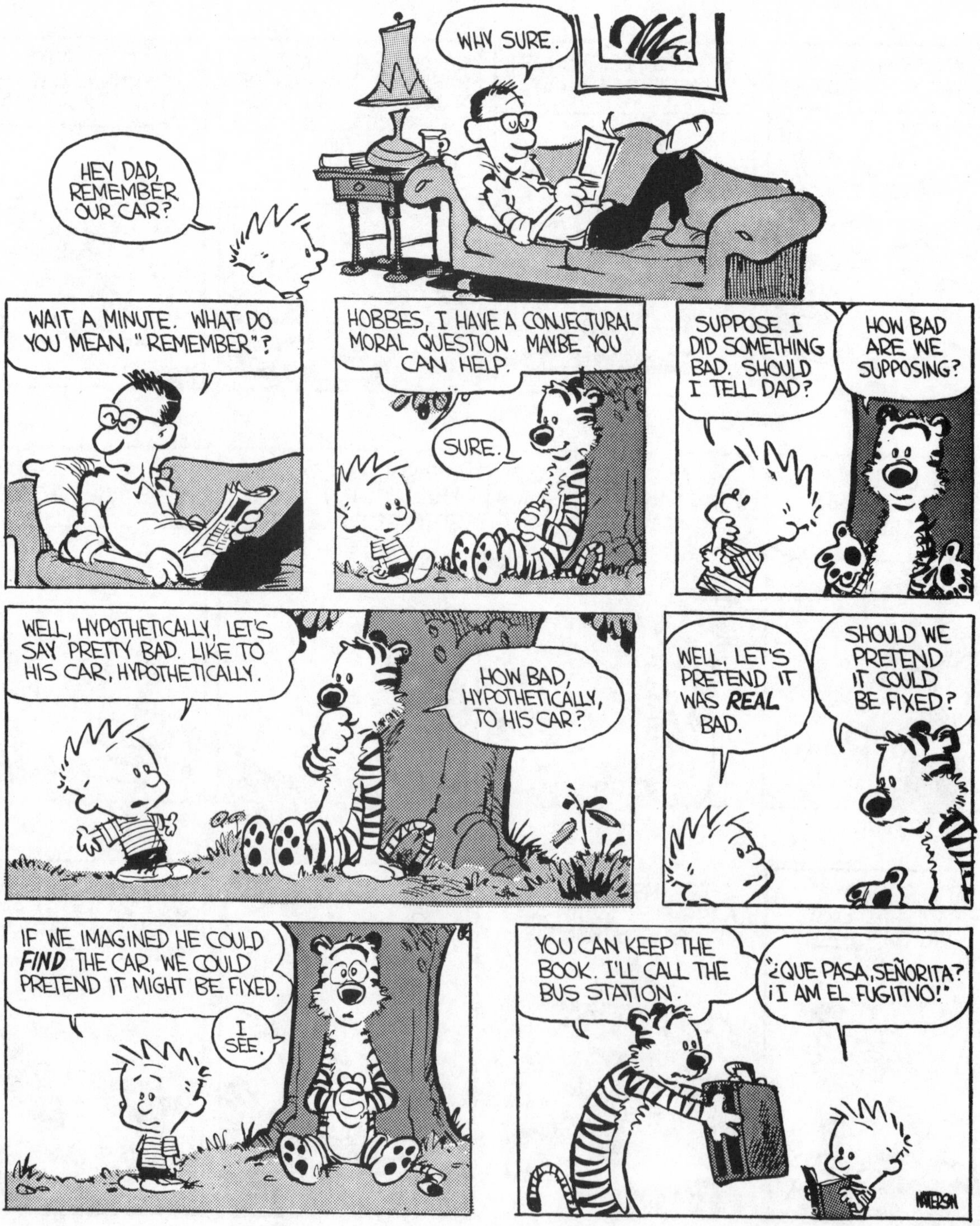
HEY DAD, REMEMBER OUR CAR?
WHY SURE.
WAIT A MINUTE. WHAT DO YOU MEAN, "REMEMBER"?
HOBBES, I HAVE A CONJECTURAL MORAL QUESTION. MAYBE YOU CAN HELP.
SURE.
SUPPOSE I DID SOMETHING BAD. SHOULD I TELL DAD?
HOW BAD ARE WE SUPPOSING?
WELL, HYPOTHETICALLY, LET'S SAY PRETTY BAD. LIKE TO HIS CAR, HYPOTHETICALLY.
HOW BAD, HYPOTHETICALLY, TO HIS CAR?
WELL, LET'S PRETEND IT WAS **REAL** BAD.
SHOULD WE PRETEND IT COULD BE FIXED?
IF WE IMAGINED HE COULD **FIND** THE CAR, WE COULD PRETEND IT MIGHT BE FIXED.
I SEE.
YOU CAN KEEP THE BOOK. I'LL CALL THE BUS STATION.
"¿QUE PASA, SEÑORITA? ¡I AM EL FUGITIVO!"
WATERSON

WHY CAN'T I STAY UP LATE? YOU GUYS CAN!
IT'S NOT FAIR!
THE WORLD ISN'T FAIR, CALVIN.
I KNOW, BUT WHY ISN'T IT EVER UNFAIR IN MY FAVOR?
WATTERSON

THE VALIANT SPACEMAN SPIFF IS BEING PURSUED BY A DISGUSTING SCUM BEING!
SPIFF SPOTS HIS HOVERING SPACESHIP AND BOLTS FOR THE LADDER!
BUT HE'S TOO LATE! THE AWFUL SCUM BEING IS UPON HIM! IT'S ALL OVER!
IT'S ALL OVER!!
I TOLD YOU THREE TIMES RECESS WAS OVER! NOW GET INSIDE!
WATTERSON

AS DICTATOR, I HAVE THE SOLE VOICE IN GOVERNMENT!
I WILL NOT TOLERATE DISSENT!
I ALONE SHALL DECIDE THE GOOD! I ALONE SHALL..
TIME FOR BED, CALVIN.
COULDN'T WE VOTE ON THIS?
WATTERSON

IF YOU COULD WISH FOR ANYTHING, WHAT WOULD IT BE?
A BIG SUNNY FIELD TO BE IN.
A STUPID FIELD?! YOU'VE GOT THAT NOW! THINK BIG! RICHES! POWER! PRETEND YOU COULD HAVE ANYTHING!
Z
ACTUALLY, IT'S HARD TO ARGUE WITH SOMEONE WHO LOOKS SO HAPPY.

HERE FISH!
THEY MUST KNOW THAT ONE.

AAGHH!
CHOMP!
ARE THE FISH BITING?
DROP DEAD, HOBBES.

OOPS! I FORGOT TO READ CHAPTER FIVE FOR SCHOOL TOMORROW.
WHAT ARE YOU GOING TO DO?
CATCH A QUICK COLD.
COUGH COUGH
YOU SOUND TERRIBLE, CALVIN. I'LL GET YOU SOME COUGH MEDICINE.
IT WASN'T ME COUGHING. IT WAS HOBBES.
ME? IT WASN'T ME!
I KNOW, BUT THAT COUGH SYRUP TASTES AWFUL.
SO YOU'RE GOING TO HAVE ME TAKE IT? NOTHING DOING, BUSTER. I REFUSE!
HERE YOU GO, CALVIN. OPEN UP.
NOT ME! GIVE IT TO HOBBES! HE'S THE ONE WHO..
GLOOMP
ACKTHP!
PBTHBBPPTH!!
HACK
HACK
MMMM! THAT COUGH MEDICINE IS GOOD! YOU SHOULD TRY SOME! REALLY!
YOU'RE NOT FOOLING ME ONE BIT, YOU STINKER.
WATTERSON

I CAN'T GET THIS MODEL AIRPLANE TO LOOK RIGHT.
THESE DIRECTIONS ARE IMPOSSIBLE!
RRRRRGGGHHHHH
WHAM
WHAM
WHAM
HIT BY ANTI-AIRCRAFT GUNS.
YOUR PLANES DO SEEM TO RUN INTO THOSE, DON'T THEY?
WATERSON

TOMMY TOLD A FUNNY STORY AT SCHOOL TODAY. I ALMOST DIED!
TELL IT TO ME.
WELL, ACTUALLY THE STORY ITSELF WASN'T SO FUNNY...
...IT WAS THE WAY HE TOLD IT.
HOW DID HE TELL IT?
HE WAS DRINKING MILK AND WHEN HE LAUGHED, IT CAME UP HIS NOSE!
WATERSON

You've got two periods to live, Twinky.
Then it's gym class, and I turn you into hamburger casserole!
I HATE GYM CLASS.
COACH THINKS VIOLENCE IS AEROBIC.
WATERSON

WHERE'S MY JACKET?
I'VE LOOKED EVERYWHERE! UNDER THE BED, OVER MY CHAIR...
...ON THE STAIRS, ON THE HALL FLOOR, IN THE KITCHEN... IT'S JUST NOT ANYWHERE!
OH, HERE IT IS! WHO PUT IT IN THE STUPID CLOSET?!?
WATERSON

HOCUS-POCUS, ABRACADABRA!
I COMMAND MY HOMEWORK TO DO ITSELF! HOMEWORK, BE DONE!
WATERSON
FLIP FLIP FLIP
RATS.

DO YOU EVER THINK ABOUT THE END OF THE WORLD AS WE KNOW IT?
YOU MEAN A NUCLEAR WAR?
WATERSON
I THINK MOM WAS REFERRING TO IF SHE EVER CATCHES ME LETTING THE AIR OUT OF THE CAR TIRES AGAIN.

I'M TAKING THE UMBRELLA OUTSIDE.
WELL, THAT'S SHOWING A LITTLE FORESIGHT FOR ONCE. GOOD FOR YOU.
WAIT A MINUTE...
YOU REALLY THINK THIS WILL WORK?
OF COURSE! LET'S GO!
SMASH!
BONK
BONK
BONK
ITY BIPPITY BIPPITY BIPPITY
LOOK! I'M FLYING!!
I HAD MY EYES SHUT. HOW WAS IT?
GREAT! WHAT A RIDE! LET'S GET SOME OTHER KIDS AND CHARGE 'EM!
WATTERSON

FEARLESS SPACEMAN SPIFF CLOSES IN ON THE FLEEING ZARGONS!
ONCE AGAIN OUR HERO IS ABOUT TO TEACH VICIOUS ALIEN SCUM THAT VIRTUE IS ITS OWN REWARD! HE LOCKS ONTO TARGET!
PSST, CALVIN! WHAT WAS THE CAPITAL OF POLAND UNTIL 1600?
KRAKOW.
THANKS.
KRAKOW! KRAKOW! TWO DIRECT HITS!

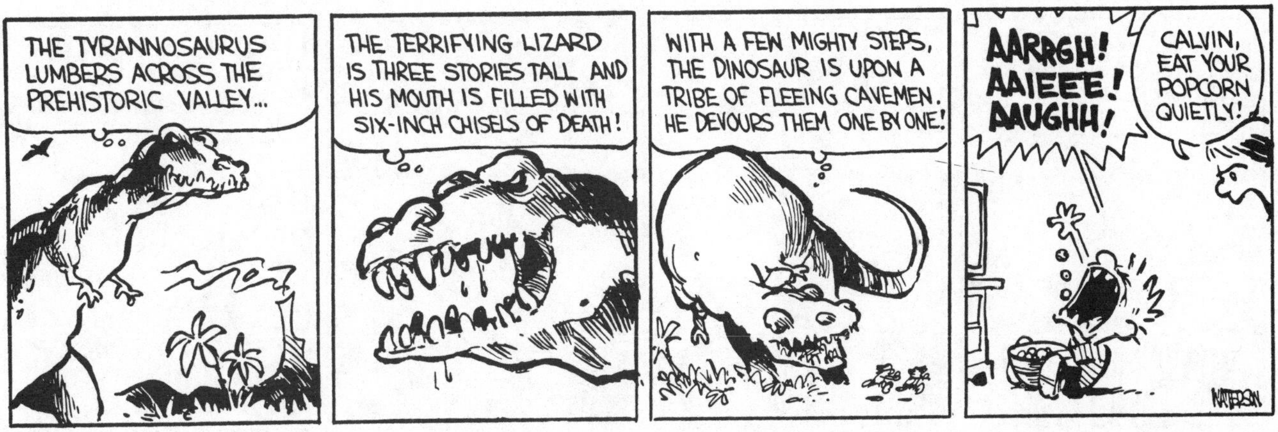
THE TYRANNOSAURUS LUMBERS ACROSS THE PREHISTORIC VALLEY...
THE TERRIFYING LIZARD IS THREE STORIES TALL AND HIS MOUTH IS FILLED WITH SIX-INCH CHISELS OF DEATH!
WITH A FEW MIGHTY STEPS, THE DINOSAUR IS UPON A TRIBE OF FLEEING CAVEMEN. HE DEVOURS THEM ONE BY ONE!
AARRGH! AAIEEE! AAUGHH!
CALVIN, EAT YOUR POPCORN QUIETLY!

WHAT DOES THIS WORD MEAN?
WHICH ONE?
THAT LONG ONE.
!
I DON'T KNOW.
YOU DO TOO!! ALL RIGHT! WHERE'S A DICTIONARY??

CAN I WATCH THE MOVIE "KILLER PROM QUEEN" ON TV ?
NO.
DO I HAVE TO EAT THIS SLIMY ASPARAGUS?
YES.
CAN I STAY UP TILL MIDNIGHT?
NO.
THERE'S AN INVERSE RELATIONSHIP BETWEEN HOW GOOD SOMETHING IS FOR YOU, AND HOW MUCH FUN IT IS.

LET'S SEE WHAT HAPPENS IF YOU COOK POPCORN WITHOUT A LID.
POW
KAPWING
POW
BANG
ZANG
BOING
HECK, THAT'S MORE FUN THAN EXPLODING A POTATO IN THE MICROWAVE!
LET'S DO SOME MORE!

C'MON, CALVIN. WE'RE GOING TO THE STORE.
CAN HOBBES COME?
NO, JUST LEAVE HIM HERE.
BUT I WANT HIM TO COME WITH US!!
IF YOU CAN'T WIN BY REASON, GO FOR VOLUME.

HONEY, WE HAVE TO LEAVE SOON. IS CALVIN TAKING HIS BATH?
OH GOOD.
WHILE I'M TAKING MY BATH, YOU CAN BRUSH YOUR TEETH AND COMB YOUR HAIR.
RIGHT.
YOUR DAD WON'T MIND IF I USE HIS COLOGNE, WILL HE?
WELL, GO EASY THIS TIME.
THINK I SHOULD SHAVE?
NO, GO FOR THE DON JOHNSON FUZZY LOOK.
HERE'S A TIE AND ONE OF MY SPORT COATS.
PERFECT! RIGHT OUT OF "GQ"!
BOY, I LOOK GOOD IN ANYTHING, DON'T I?
REFRESH MY MEMORY. ***HOW*** DID I GET TALKED INTO THIS ONE?
MY FRIEND WOULD LIKE TO SEE THE WINE LIST.
WATTERSON

SO THE CONTRACTOR SAYS IT WILL COST ABOUT $200 TO FIX.
OH, THAT DUMB KID!
WELL, IT'S ALL PART OF RAISING A CHILD, RIGHT?
MM.
YOU'RE NOT SORRY WE HAD CALVIN, ARE YOU?
ARE YOU?
I ASKED FIRST.... BESIDES, IT WASN'T ALL MY DECISION.
ALL I KNOW IS THAT I OFFERED TO BUY US A DACHSHUND, BUT NO, YOU SAID...

DO YOU THINK THERE'S A GOD?
WELL SOMEBODY'S OUT TO GET ME.

SPACEMAN SPIFF CLOSES IN ON THE ALIEN VESSEL!
THE ALIEN, BEING UNNATURALLY STUPID, IS BLISSFULLY IGNORANT OF ITS IMMINENT DOOM!
OUR HERO LOCKS ONTO TARGET AND WARMS UP HIS FRAP-RAY BLASTER!
MISS WORMWOOD!!
ZOUNDS! A GORKON DEATH STATION APPEARS! EVASIVE ACTION!

WHACK!
WOW! ANOTHER HOLE IN ONE!

WOW! THREE NEW MAGAZINES FOR ME TODAY.
YESTERDAY I GOT FIVE. I LOVE GETTING ALL THIS MAIL.
HOW COME YOU RECEIVE ALL THESE MAGAZINES?
I WENT TO THE LIBRARY AND FILLED OUT ALL THE SUBSCRIPTION CARDS THAT SAID "BILL ME LATER."

I LOVE SATURDAY MORNING CARTOONS.
WHAT CLASSIC HUMOR!
THIS IS WHAT ENTERTAINMENT IS ALL ABOUT.
... IDIOTS, EXPLOSIVES, AND FALLING ANVILS.

WANNA GO CATCH SOME FISH?
SURE.
UGH. I DON'T WANT TO TOUCH THESE WORMS. WILL YOU PUT ONE ON MY HOOK?
ME? I'M NOT GONNA SPEAR ANY WORMS!
I KNOW... LET'S JUST DUMP THE WORMS IN THE WATER, AND WHEN THE FISH COME UP TO EAT THEM, WE'LL CATCH THEM IN THE NET!
PRETTY SMART, HUH? THAT'S WHAT I LIKE ABOUT SURVIVING IN THE WILD—PITTING OUR WITS AGAINST THE RAGING ELEMENTS!
THE WORMS ARE GETTING SOGGY.
OOH, THEY'RE STARTING TO SINK.
BLIP
BLOOP
BLORP
LET'S PIT OUR WITS AGAINST SOME FAST FOOD CHEESEBURGERS. THOSE COME IN NEAT LITTLE BOXES.
YEAH, WHO'D WANT TO EAT SOMETHING THAT EATS WORMS ANYWAY?
WATTERSON

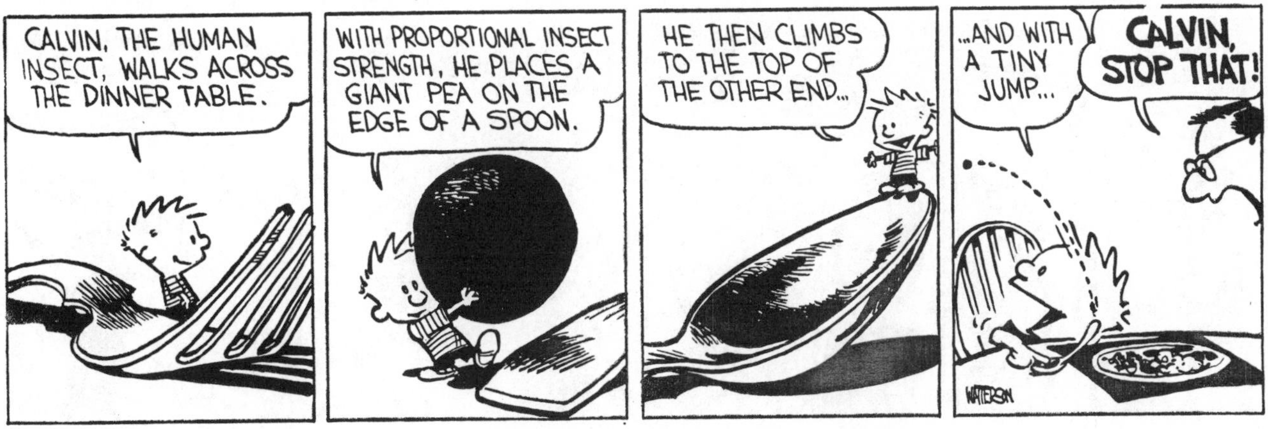
CALVIN, THE HUMAN INSECT, WALKS ACROSS THE DINNER TABLE.
WITH PROPORTIONAL INSECT STRENGTH, HE PLACES A GIANT PEA ON THE EDGE OF A SPOON.
HE THEN CLIMBS TO THE TOP OF THE OTHER END...
...AND WITH A TINY JUMP...
CALVIN, STOP THAT!
WATTERSON

IN HIS MINUSCULE SIZE, IT TAKES CALVIN, THE HUMAN INSECT, TEN MINUTES TO WALK ACROSS A BOOK'S PAGE!
AT THE OTHER END, HE SLOWLY LIFTS THE GIGANTIC SHEET!
95
THEN IT'S ANOTHER TEN-MINUTE JOURNEY BACK, AS HE TURNS IT OVER!
GEE, THE KID'S BEEN QUIET FOR ALMOST TWENTY MINUTES.
HE'S DOING HIS HOMEWORK.
WATTERSON

HERE'S A MOVIE WE SHOULD WATCH.
WHO'S IN IT?
IT SAYS, "JAPANESE CAST."
WATTERSON
"TWO BIG RUBBERY MONSTERS SLUG IT OUT OVER MAJOR METROPOLITAN CENTERS IN A BATTLE FOR WORLD SUPREMACY."
DOESN'T THAT SOUND GREAT?
AND PEOPLE SAY THAT FOREIGN FILM IS INACCESSIBLE.

OH, ROSALYN, YOU'RE HERE! GOOD, COME IN!
WE REALLY APPRECIATE YOUR COMING ON SUCH SHORT NOTICE. WE'VE HAD A TERRIBLE TIME GETTING A BABY SITTER FOR TONIGHT.
HA HA, MAYBE LITTLE CALVIN HERE HAS GOTTEN HIMSELF A REPUTATION.
HA HA. YOU HAVE THE HALF UP FRONT?
YES, LET ME GET MY PURSE...
HI, BABY DOLL, IT'S ME. YEAH, I'M BABY SITTING THE KID DOWN THE STREET.
YEAH, THAT'S RIGHT, THE LITTLE MONSTER. ... HMM?... WELL SO FAR, NO PROBLEM.
HE HASN'T BEEN ANY TROUBLE. YOU JUST HAVE TO SHOW THESE KIDS WHO'S THE BOSS. ..MM HMM..
HOW MUCH LONGER TILL SHE LETS US OUT OF THE GARAGE?
SHE SAID 8 O'CLOCK, AND IT'S ALMOST 6:30 NOW...
THANKS AGAIN FOR BABY SITTING, ROSALYN.
CALVIN WAS NO TROUBLE AT ALL.
THAT'S GOOD. I'LL GET THE CAR AND DRIVE YOU HOME.
THERE YOU GO. GOOD NIGHT.
THANK YOU. GOOD NIGHT.
IS SHE GONE?

WE'VE GOT A BABY SITTER TONIGHT.
READY?
READY.
CALVIN, THE BABY SITTER IS HERE! WE'RE GOING! BE GOOD, OK?
HI THERE. YOU MUST BE CALVIN.
HMMPH.
YOU'RE NOT MY MOM, SO I DON'T HAVE TO DO ANYTHING YOU SAY. I'M GOING TO DO WHATEVER I FEEL LIKE, SO JUST STAY OUT OF THE WAY.
CALVIN, TAKE A LOOK BY THE TELEPHONE AND TELL ME WHAT YOU SEE.
A NOTE MOM LEFT WITH EMERGENCY NUMBERS.
RIGHT. NOW YOU WOULDN'T WANT ME TO HAVE TO **CALL** ANY OF THOSE NUMBERS, WOULD YOU?
WELL, IT MUST BE 6:30. GUESS I'LL TURN IN.
FOR EIGHT BUCKS A NIGHT, I DON'T PUT UP WITH MUCH.
WATTERSON

WHAT A GREAT NIGHT TO CAMP OUT!
WHERE'S OUR TENT? I THOUGHT THE SCOUTMASTER SAID TO SET THEM UP.
UH OH.
WHEN HE SAID TO PITCH THE TENT, I THREW IT AWAY.

THE BEST PART ABOUT THESE HIKES IS GETTING TO SEE SO MUCH WILDLIFE.
LOOK! A TIGER!
A TIGER?!
DON'T **DO** THAT!

WE'RE SEPARATED FROM THE TROOP AND HOPELESSLY LOST!
LEFT ALONE IN THE UNCOMPROMISING WILD TO SURVIVE BY OUR WITS UNAIDED!
HEY, DUMMY! THE SCOUTMASTER SAYS TO GRAB YOUR STUPID STUFFED TIGER AND GET YOUR REAR IN GEAR!
WE'LL TRY TO LOSE 'EM AGAIN OVER THE NEXT HILL.

GRAB THE HOTDOGS AND COME ON!
THE TROOP'S COOKING DINNER OVER THE FIRE.
OH THAT'S JUST GREAT.
HERE WE'VE BEEN LUGGING THIS DUMB MICROWAVE AROUND FOR NOTHING.

BOP
SPIKE!
OH OH, WE'D BETTER LEAVE!
IT LOOKS LIKE SOME BIG PEOPLE WANT TO PLAY TENNIS.

THE CROCODILE FLOATS TO THE TOP OF THE MURKY AMAZON...
COMPLETELY MOTIONLESS, HE APPEARS TO BE ONLY A HARMLESS LOG.
A HIPPOPOTAMUS APPROACHES AND ENSURES ITS INSTANT DEATH!
CALVIN, WHAT ARE YOU DOING? ARE YOU ALL RIGHT?
CLOSER... CLOSER...

LOOK, IT SAYS YOU HAVE TO BE EIGHTEEN TO BUY CIGARETTES.
EIGHTEEN?!? BY THEN I'LL KNOW BETTER!
MOM, CAN I HAVE A CIGARETTE?
SURE, CALVIN. I THINK YOUR GRANDFATHER LEFT SOME HERE. JUST SMOKE OUTSIDE, OK?
WOW!
YOUR MOM LET YOU HAVE A CIGARETTE?
FOR A MOM, SOMETIMES SHE'S PRETTY COOL.
EEEEEEP
BLAAUGH!
GAG
HACK
COUGH
YOU'D THINK THIS WOULD BE AN EASY HABIT TO BREAK.
WHEEZE
ACK
WATERSON
WELL NOW... DID WE LEARN A LITTLE LESSON TODAY?
*GASP* ..YES...
TRUSTING PARENTS CAN BE HAZARDOUS TO YOUR HEALTH.

MOM! MOM! A BIG DOG KNOCKED ME DOWN AND HE STOLE HOBBES!
I TRIED TO CATCH HIM, BUT I COULDN'T, AND NOW I'VE LOST MY BEST FRIEND!
WELL CALVIN, IF YOU WOULDN'T DRAG THAT TIGER EVERYWHERE, THINGS LIKE THIS WOULDN'T HAPPEN.
THERE'S NO PROBLEM SO AWFUL THAT YOU CAN'T ADD SOME GUILT TO IT AND MAKE IT EVEN WORSE!

I CAN'T SLEEP AT ALL. POOR HOBBES! I WONDER WHERE HE IS. I HOPE HE'S OK.
*SNIFF*.. WHAT DID I EVER DO TO DESERVE THIS?
WHATEVER IT WAS, I'M SORRY ALREADY!

Lost: My tiGER, "HobbES"
MAYBE YOU SHOULD DESCRIBE HIM.
ON tHE QUIEt sidE. SOMEwhat PECuLiaR. A GOod ComPaNION, iN a WEIRd SoRt of Way.
I MEAN, WHAT DOES HE LOOK LIKE?
OH.

WELL LOOK, SOMEBODY LEFT A STUFFED TIGER OUT IN THE FIELD. HOW STRANGE.
LOOKS LIKE A DOG'S BEEN CHEWING ON YOU, FELLA.
WELL, NOTHING A LITTLE TEA PARTY WITH SOME OTHER STUFFED ANIMALS WOULDN'T HELP. C'MON.

HOBBES! HOBBES! WHERE ARE YOU ?!?
HELLO, CALVIN. WOULD YOU LIKE TO JOIN MY TEA PARTY?
HECK NO. I'M TRYING TO FIND MY BEST FRIEND, WHO'S BEEN KIDNAPPED BY A DOG. LEAVE ME ALONE.
WELL I THINK MR. CALVIN IS VERY RUDE, DON'T YOU, MR. TIGER? YES, I THINK SO TOO. MORE TEA, ANYONE?

HEY, I SHOULD TELL SUSIE TO KEEP HER EYES OPEN FOR HOBBES.
SUSIE, I...
HOBBES!
YOU FOUND HOBBES! THANK YOU THANK YOU THANKYOUTHANKYOUTHANKY OUTHANKYOUTHANKYOUTHA
WELL! WASN'T MR. CALVIN A GENTLEMAN! I DO HOPE... HEY! WHO TOOK ALL THE COOKIES ?!?

WHAT'S THAT SMELL?
EITHER MOM'S COOKING DINNER, OR SOMEBODY GOT SICK IN THE FURNACE DUCT.
BOY, DOES IT STINK IN HERE! WHAT ARE YOU COOKING FOR DINNER?!
WHATEVER IT IS, I'M NOT EATING IT.
I'M STEWING SOME MONKEY HEADS.
MONKEY HEADS?
THEY'LL BE SOGGY ENOUGH TO EAT IN ABOUT TWENTY MINUTES.
REALLY?? WE'RE HAVING MONKEY HEADS? WE ARE NOT. ...ARE THOSE REALLY MONKEY HEADS?
WOW! MONKEY HEADS!
I'VE NEVER HAD MONKEY HEADS BEFORE! I WONDER WHAT THEY'RE LIKE.
WATERSON
MM...KINDA SQUISHY. OOH LOOK, IS THAT A NOSE? WHAT'S THIS? BRAINS? I DIDN'T THINK THEY'D BE SO RUBBERY...
WHAT? I THOUGHT THESE WERE STUFFED PEPPERS. HONEY, WHAT THE HECK IS THIS?? WHATEVER IT IS, I'M NOT EATING IT!

SUSIE, WANNA HEAR A SECRET?
SURE.
I THINK THE PRINCIPAL IS A SPACE ALIEN SPY.
HE'S TRYING TO CORRUPT OUR YOUNG INNOCENT MINDS SO WE'LL BE UNABLE TO RESIST WHEN HIS PEOPLE INVADE EARTH!
PROMISE NOT TO TELL ANYONE?
DON'T WORRY.

HOBBES, WHAT SHOULD I DO WHEN MOE COMES TO BEAT ME UP IN GYM CLASS?
WELL, YOU CAN ALWAYS DO WHAT WE TIGERS DO WHEN A RHINO CHARGES.
WHAT'S THAT?
WE SCRAMBLE LIKE MANIACS FOR THE NEAREST TREE.
THAT'S YOUR ADVICE?? TO SIT IN A TREE ALL DAY?!?
IT DOESN'T IMPRESS THE GIRLS, OF COURSE, BUT THERE'S NO SENSE IMPRESSING THEM AND THEN GETTING KILLED, MY DAD USED TO SAY...

HOBBES, I NEED YOUR HELP. THAT BULLY MOE KEEPS PUSHING ME AROUND.
...SO I WANT YOU TO COME TO SCHOOL AND EAT HIM, OK?
EAT HIM?
SURE! TIGERS EAT PEOPLE ALL THE TIME!
WHAT IF THE CAFETERIA LADIES WON'T LET ME USE THE OVEN?

IT'S TOO EARLY TO BE IN BED. IT'S HARDLY EVEN DARK OUT. WHY DO I HAVE TO BE IN BED? IT'S RIDICULOUS.
I'M NOT EVEN TIRED! I DON'T NEED TO BE IN BED! THIS IS AN OUTRAGE!
IT'S THE STUPIDEST THING I CAN IMAGINE! I THINK MOM AND DAD ARE JUST TRYING TO GET RID OF ME. I CAN'T SLEEP AT ALL. CAN YOU SLEEP, HOBBES?
NO!

OK, MOM, HOBBES AND I HAVE FORMED A LOBBY. WE WANT MORE PRIVILEGES!
MORE PRIVILEGES? LIKE WHAT? YOU'VE GOT IT MADE!
NO RESPONSIBILITIES, NO CARES, NO WORRIES! WHAT MORE COULD YOU POSSIBLY WANT?
WHY DIDN'T YOU TELL HER ABOUT THE CREDIT CARDS IN OUR NAMES?
YOU HEARD HER. SHE'S IN ONE OF HER MOODS.

I LOVE SATURDAYS!
EVERY SATURDAY I GET UP AT SIX AND EAT THREE BOWLS OF CRUNCHY SUGAR BOMBS.
THEN I WATCH CARTOONS TILL NOON, AND I'M INCOHERENT AND HYPERACTIVE THE REST OF THE DAY.
DOES IT WORK?
NO BROTHERS OR SISTERS **SO** FAR!

NO EARTHLING HAS EVER BEFORE SEEN THE CRATERED, SCARRED SURFACE OF DISTANT PLANET ZOG!
WE JOIN THE FEARLESS SPACEMAN SPIFF, INTERPLANETARY EXPLORER EXTRAORDINAIRE, OUT AT THE FARTHEST REACHES OF THE GALAXY...
... ALTHOUGH IT'S NOT UNLIKE SOME OF THOSE ZIT CREAM COMMERCIALS...
WITH NERVES OF STEEL, OUR HERO SETS FORTH ON HIS DANGEROUS MISSION!
HE FIRES HIS HYPER-JETS AND...
...BLASTS INTO THE FIFTH DIMENSION!
INTO A WORLD BEYOND HUMAN COMPREHENSION!
INTO A WORLD WHERE TIME HAS NO MEANING!
WATTERSON
MAN, THIS CLASS LASTS FOREVER!
SO WE CARRY THE THREE INTO THE TENS COLUMN....

IN THE COMMERCIALS, THIS COLA GREATLY INCREASES ONE'S SEX APPEAL.
GLIK
GLIK
GLICK
GLIGK
BUR-UR-URPP!!
EVIDENTLY A LITTLE LICENSE ON MADISON AVENUE'S PART.
PHOO! RIGHT UP MY NOSE.
WATERSON

IT'S AN OUTRAGE THAT SIX-YEAR-OLDS CAN'T VOTE!
HERE I AM, A U.S. CITIZEN, WITH NO VOICE IN OUR REPRESENTATIVE GOVERNMENT!
YOU'RE CONCERNED ABOUT THE DIRECTION THE COUNTRY IS HEADED?
NO, I JUST WANT A BIGGER PIECE OF THE PIE.
WATERSON

Dad PERFORMANCE

HERE, CALVIN, I'LL SHOW YOU A MAGIC TRICK.
SEE? I PULLED A DIME FROM YOUR EAR! PRETTY GOOD, HUH?
ANYTHING YET?
J-JUST A B-B-BLOODY N-NOSE.
WATTERSON

POOF
POOF
POOF
POW!
GOOD HEAVENS, I THINK I BLEW MY FACE INSIDE OUT!
WATTERSON

TRESUR MAP
X

THE WATER'S TOO COLD!
NOW IT'S TOO HOT.
NOW IT'S TOO COLD.
NOW IT'S TOO DEEP.

THE FEARSOME SHARK SENSES DISTRESS IN THE WAVES ABOVE HIM!
HE CIRCLES UP, CLOSER AND CLOSER TO THE TERRIFIED VICTIM!
HEY!
YAHH!
SNAP
THRASH
SNAP
YOU KNOW, FOR SOMEONE WHO HATES BATHS AS MUCH AS YOU DO, YOU'RE NOT MAKING THIS GO ANY FASTER!
ANOTHER GRUESOME KILL..

WE SHOULD MAKE DAD A FATHER'S DAY CARD.
OKAY, I'LL DRAW A PICTURE OF HIM ON IT.
HMM... MAKE HIS MOUTH BIGGER. HE USUALLY LOOKS ANGRIER THAN THAT.
GOOD MORNING, DAD! HAPPY FATHER'S DAY!
MMF. GOOMRG.
IN APPRECIATION OF YOUR SERVICE AS DAD, TODAY I AM LIVING ACCORDING TO THE PRINCIPLES OF YOUR FATHERLY WISDOM.
CALVIN, WHAT TIME IS...
FIVE IN THE MORNING?!
YES, "EARLY TO BED, EARLY TO RISE," YOU ALWAYS SAY...
I WAS GOING TO BUY YOU A NICE PRESENT, BUT "A PENNY SAVED IS A PENNY EARNED," AS YOU SAY...
..SO I'M NOW EARNING 6% ON THE MONEY I DIDN'T SPEND.
YES, DAD, THANKS TO YOU, I'M A HAPPIER, BETTER PERSON.
GOOD WORK, SOCRATES.
I KNEW WE'D MADE A MISTAKE THE MINUTE I SAW THAT LITTLE BOLOGNA LOAF IN THE HOSPITAL BASSINET.
WATERSON

I'VE NEVER BEEN THIS HIGH IN A TREE BEFORE.
ME EITHER. YOU CAN SEE FOR MILES FROM UP HERE.
I'LL SAY! I'M GLAD WE'RE UP HERE.
THAT WAS QUITE A CRASH, WASN'T IT?

THE RAIN STOPPED!
THIS IS THE BEST TIME TO GO WORMUCKING. LET'S GO!
WHAT'S THAT?
IT'S WHEN YOU WALK ON THE PAVEMENT AND MUCK ALL THE WORMS.

CALVIN, QUIT CHARGING AROUND THE HOUSE!!
BINK
BONK
BOOM
WHAT DID I JUST TELL YOU?!?
BEATS ME. WEREN'T YOU LISTENING EITHER?

BANG! YOU'RE DEAD!
NO I'M NOT. YOU MISSED!
I DID NOT! YOU CHEATER!
I'M HERE TALKING TO YOU, AREN'T I?
OK, THEN.. BANG!
MY, WHAT A MISERABLE SHOT YOU ARE!
WATTERSON

HURRY UP, CALVIN. OUR RESERVATION IS FOR 7:00.
CAN HOBBES COME TO THE RESTAURANT?
NO.
WHY NOT?
WE'RE AFRAID HE MIGHT EAT SOMEONE. LET'S GO.
THAT'S RIGHT. YOU PROBABLY *WOULD*, WOULDN'T YOU?
I CAN NEVER STAY ON A DIET IN A RESTAURANT.

ARR! LOOK ALIVE, YE SCURVY SCALLIWAGS! THAR'S A FRIGATE TO BOARD!
RUN UP THE SKULL AND CROSSBONES!
PREPARE THE PLANK!
WATTERSON
OUR SHIP **IS** A PLANK.
AND YOU'RE GOING TO WALK IT, WISE GUY!

PTOO!
BLAT
WAP
THOK
BONK!
POOM
WUNK
NICE DOUBLE PLAY. WHO'S OUT?
IT DEPENDS. ARE YOU ON MY TEAM, OR AM I ON YOUR TEAM?
WATTERSON

A BEE LANDED ON YOUR BACK!
A BEE?! ACCKK! GET IT AWAY!!
DON'T MOVE, AND IT WON'T STING YOU.
JUST STAND STILL AND TRY NOT TO IMAGINE THAT IT MIGHT VERY WELL CRAWL DOWN YOUR SHIRT AND INTO YOUR PANTS!
YOWW!
HE IMAGINED IT.
WATTERSON

OK, LET'S FLUSH IT!
FLUSH
HA HA HA
HA
WHIZZZZ
HA
WATTERSON
HEE HEE! THAT WAS GREAT! LET'S DO IT AGAIN!
FLUSH
I DON'T WANT TO KNOW WHAT HE'S DOING. DO YOU?
NO. LET'S GO CHECK.

I'VE HAD TROUBLE CHOOSING A NEW HOBBY.
FIRST I WANTED TO COLLECT BUGS.
THEN I WANTED TO COLLECT STAMPS.
WHAT DID YOU DECIDE ON?
STAMPED BUGS.
WATTERSON

EVERYBODY I KNOW HAS EITHER CABLE TV OR A VCR! THEY CAN WATCH ANYTHING THEY WANT!
BUT ME? I HAVE TO WATCH DUMB OL' SUMMER REPEATS! I HAVE TO WATCH THE SAME GARBAGE OVER AND OVER!
HOW CRUELLY WE MISTREAT YOU, CALVIN.
...SO THEN HE GAVE ME "OLIVER TWIST" TO READ, AND SAID I MIGHT IDENTIFY WITH IT.
RATS...AND "SORORITY ROW HORROR" IS ON CABLE TONIGHT.
WATTERSON

I GOT A HELIUM BALLOON.
VERY NICE.
I'M GOING TO STAND ON THIS LADDER AND LET THE BALLOON CARRY ME UP AND AWAY.
NOTHING'S HAPPENING.
TRY JUMPING.
SEE? THERE GOES THE BALLOON. YOU DIDN'T HANG ON.
WATTERSON

WATTERSON
FLUSH!
WHEEE! HA HA HA!
I'M DONE WITH MY BATH.
MM... THAT WAS QUICK.

CALVIN, QUIT HORSING AROUND!
HOBBES IS CROWDING ME.
THIS IS MY HALF OF THE SEAT, GOT IT, STRIPEYPANTS? THAT'S YOUR SIDE! YOU STAY OVER THERE!
I SEE THAT!!
CALVIN, I'M TRYING TO CONCENTRATE. BE QUIET.
HOBBES POKED ME.
I DON'T CARE WHAT HOBBES DID! JUST BE QUIET UNTIL WE GET OUT OF THIS TRAFFIC.
HEE HEE! (STOP IT. YOU HEARD DAD!)
GKKPT! PTHB!
HOO HOO! GKPTHB! (WE'RE GONNA GET IN TROUBLE!)
HEE HEE
MMP MP! (SHHHH!) HEE HEE!
WATTERSON
HEE HOO HA HEE
HA HA
HO HA
CALVIN! I THOUGHT I SAID I WANTED IT QUIET!!
WE WERE HAVING A WEIRD FACE CONTEST, DAD, BUT WE'RE ALL THROUGH NOW.
YOU WON.

WHAT'S ALL THE RUCKUS?! YOU'RE SUPPOSED TO BE ASLEEP!
AND WHAT'S WITH ALL THESE FEATHERS?! ARE YOU TEARING UP YOUR PILLOWS?!
IT WAS INCREDIBLE, DAD! A HERD OF DUCKS FLEW IN THE WINDOW AND MOLTED! THEY LEFT WHEN THEY HEARD YOU COMING! HONEST!
NICE ALIBI, FRIZZLETOP! NO DESSERT FOR A WEEK!
YOU WANT ANOTHER PILLOW ACROSS THE KISSER? I DIDN'T HEAR YOU OFFER ANY BRAINSTORMS!

YOU SEE, HOBBES, I HAVE A WATER BALLOON, AND YOU DON'T.
I THEREFORE HAVE OFFENSIVE SUPERIORITY, SO YOU HAVE TO DO WHAT I SAY. WHAT DO YOU THINK OF THAT?
I THINK I'LL TAKE THIS STICK AND POKE YOUR BALLOON.
THAT'S THE TROUBLE WITH WEAPONS TECHNOLOGY. IT BECOMES OBSOLETE SO QUICKLY.

OH MY GOSH, HOBBES! DON'T MOVE!
WHAT? WHAT IS IT?
THE BIGGEST, UGLIEST, FUZZIEST CATERPILLAR I'VE EVER SEEN IS ABOUT TO CHOMP YOUR BOTTOM!
AAUGH! KILL IT! KILL IT!
YOWW!
WHAM!
YOU KNOW WHAT YOUR PROBLEM IS? YOU'VE GOT NO APPRECIATION FOR PHYSICAL HUMOR, THAT'S WHAT!

WHERE ARE YOU GOING?
I'M GOING TO WALK TO THE OTHER SIDE OF THE LAKE.
WHAT'S THE BUCKET FOR?
TO DRAIN THE LAKE.
WATTERSON

YOU KNOW WHAT I LIKE ABOUT SUMMER DAYS?
THEY'RE JUST MADE FOR DOING THINGS.
...EVEN IF IT'S NOTHING.
ESPECIALLY IF IT'S NOTHING.
WATTERSON

THIS LOOKS LIKE A GREAT PLACE TO CATCH A CRAWDAD.
WHAT WILL WE DO WITH IT IF WE CATCH ONE?
WELL THAT'S ONE THING WE DON'T NEED TO WORRY ABOUT.
YOU DON'T KNOW WHAT ONE IS EITHER, HUH?
WATTERSON

HOBBES, YOU DIDN'T BRING YOUR SWIM TRUNKS HERE TO THE BEACH!
NO, I PREFER "FURRY DIPPING."
YAAAAAYY!
OW OW OW HOT HOT HOT HOT
AAAAAHHHHHHH
SPLOOP
SPLOP
BBBRRRR! COLD COLD COLD
OW OW OW HOT HOT HOT HOT HOT
DON'T TELL ME WE DROVE AN HOUR AND A HALF FOR THIS!
WATTERSON

WHEN ARE WE GOING TO GET TO OUR VACATION SITE? I WANNA BE THERE!
CALVIN, IT'S AN EIGHT-HOUR DRIVE. WE'RE NOT EVEN OUT OF OUR STATE YET. IT'S GOING TO BE A WHILE. RELAX.
WATTERSON
HOW MUCH LONGER NOW?
I TOLD YOU WE SHOULD HAVE FLOWN.

THERE'S A RESTAURANT COMING UP. WANT TO STOP?
ONLY IF THEY HAVE HAMBURGERS.
HAMBURGERS? THAT'S ALL WE'VE EATEN THIS WHOLE STUPID TRIP! HAMBURGERS, HAMBURGERS, HAMBURGERS!
WATTERSON
I'M SICK OF HAMBURGERS! WE'RE EATING SOMETHING ELSE FOR ONCE!
TEN MILLION BOTTLES OF BEER ON THE WALL, TEN MILLION BOTTLES OF BEER...
OK! OK! HERE'S A HAMBURGER JOINT! ARE YOU HAPPY?!

I HAVE TO GO TO THE BATHROOM.
CALVIN, WE JUST PULLED OUT OF THE RESTAURANT. CAN'T YOU WAIT? THINK OF SOMETHING ELSE.
WATTERSON
ALL I CAN THINK OF IS NIAGARA FALLS, AND THE HOOVER DAM, AND NOAH'S ARK, AND...
OOH BOY, NOW I HAVE TO GO!
NEXT YEAR I SWEAR I'LL JUST TAKE A VACATION BY MYSELF.

THAT TRIP WAS EXCRUCIATING. THANK GOODNESS WE'RE HERE.
EIGHT HOURS CRAMMED IN A CAR WITH A HYPERACTIVE SIX-YEAR-OLD! WHAT AN ORDEAL!
WATTERSON
WELL, NOW CALVIN CAN RUN AND SCREAM ALL HE LIKES. AHH, WHAT A GREAT LITTLE PLACE.
I'M BORED. WHEN ARE WE LEAVING?
YOU'RE BORED? WOULD YOU LIKE ME TO SHOW YOU HOW AN ANCHOR WORKS?

AHH! ANOTHER GLORIOUS SUNRISE, AND NOT A SOUL AROUND!
THIS IS THE LIFE! A BRISK SWIM AT DAWN, A MORNING OUT IN A BOAT...
...AND BY 9A.M., I'M BACK WITH FRESHLY CAUGHT FISH FOR BREAKFAST! THE DAY'S HARDLY BEGUN! WHAT A VACATION!
WATTERSON
UGH...I'VE SEEN CHEERIER FACES AT THE OFFICE!
YOU EAT YOUR DEAD ANIMALS. ALL I WANT IS SOME COFFEE.
WHY ISN'T THERE ANY TV UP HERE? I HATE THIS PLACE.

DAD, LOOK! I CAUGHT A FISH!
HEY, THAT'S A BIG ONE. I'LL SHOW YOU HOW TO CLEAN IT, AND WE'LL HAVE IT FOR DINNER.
"CLEAN IT"?
CUT OFF ITS HEAD AND GUT IT.
WATTERSON
MMM! PASS ME ANOTHER OF THESE GREAT CHEESE SANDWICHES! HA HA, NO BONES IN THESE, RIGHT?

GUESS WHAT'S SHORT AND UGLY AND WET ALL OVER! ...GIVE UP?
THE ANSWER HAD BETTER NOT BE WHAT I THINK IT IS...
SQUIRT SQUIRT SQUIRT SQUIRT SQUIRT SQUIRT
YOW!!
SQUIRT SQUIRT SQUIRT
BANG BONK BING
CALVIN!
IF YOU'RE GOING TO TEAR AROUND, DO IT OUTSIDE!!
OKAY, OKAY...

WOW, LOOK DOWN THERE! I THINK THAT'S THE DIM OUTLINE OF A WHALE!
I THINK THAT'S A ROCK.
AND THAT MUST BE A GIANT EEL SLITHERING UP FROM THE BOTTOM!
I THINK THAT'S A WEED.
I'LL BET THIS IS THE MAST OF AN OLD SPANISH GALLEON, SUNK HUNDREDS OF YEARS AGO.
IT'S A BRANCH.
MAN, THIS IS BORING. I WISH THERE WAS A MOVIE THEATER SOMEPLACE.
WATTERSON

WANT TO GO FISHING?
SURE.
FISHING IS ONE SPORT I REALLY LIKE.
I CAN SEE WHY... IT'S SO CONTEMPLATIVE.
THERE'S ANOTHER ONE!!
WATTERSON

GZZZZZZZZZZZ
WAAAUUGHHH!
SPLOOSH
WATTERSON

STOMP
STOMP
STOMP
STOMP
WHAP
WHAP
WHAP
WHAP
I DON'T LIKE FOOD COOKED OUT, DO YOU?
UGH. IT ALL TASTES THE SAME.
CRUNCH
CRUNCH

FLOWERS ARE PRETTY STUPID.
SEE, IT'S A BRIGHT, SUNNY DAY OUT, RIGHT?
WELL, WITH THIS WATERING CAN, I CAN MAKE THEM THINK IT'S RAINING.
IT'S FUN TO MESS WITH THEIR MINDS.

THE EXPERIMENT HAS GONE HORRIBLY WRONG! CALVIN HAS MUTATED INTO A GIANT FLY!
HE ZIPS ABOUT IN PARASITIC HUNGER, SEARCHING FOR DECAYING FLESH!
AN UNBEARABLE STENCH FILLS THE AIR. THE HIDEOUS BUG ZEROES IN.
MMM! THIS MAKES ME HUNGRY!
DON'T BE GROSS. JUST TAKE OUT THE GARBAGE LIKE I ASKED YOU, WILL YOU PLEASE?

IT'S ANOTHER NEW MORNING FOR MR. MONROE. HE GLANCES AT THE NEWSPAPER HEADLINES OVER A CUP OF COFFEE, AND GETS IN HIS RED SPORTS CAR TO GO TO WORK.
LITTLE DOES HE REALIZE IT'S HIS LAST DAY ON THE FACE OF THE EARTH!
CALVIN DRINKS THE MAGIC ELIXIR AND BEGINS AN INCREDIBLE TRANSFORMATION!
INSTANTLY HE GROWS! BIGGER AND BIGGER! HIGHER AND HIGHER!
HE IS NOW OVER 300 FEET TALL! THE FORMULA IS A SUCCESS!
CALVIN, THE MIGHTY GIANT, GOES ON A TERRIBLE RAMPAGE, STRIKING FEAR INTO THE HEARTS OF THE POPULACE!
NOTHING CAN STOP HIM! IT'S PANIC IN THE STREETS! A TOWN LIES IN RUINS!
NO, I WON'T BUY YOU ANY MORE TOY CARS. I SAW YOU! YOU DELIBERATELY STOMPED ON THOSE!
WATTERSON

C'MON, CALVIN! I SIGNED YOU UP FOR SWIMMING LESSONS.
I DON'T WANT SWIMMING LESSONS!!
TOO LATE. LET'S GO.
WHAT ABOUT HOBBES? DID YOU SIGN HIM UP TOO?
NO, IT'S NOT GOOD TO GET TIGERS WET.
WHY IS THAT?
IT TAKES US ALL DAY TO DRY, AND UNTIL WE DO, WE SMELL FUNNY.
WATERSON

I CAN'T BELIEVE MY MOM SIGNED ME UP FOR SWIMMING LESSONS.
HERE I AM FREEZING MY BUNS OFF AT 9 IN THE MORNING, ABOUT TO JUMP INTO ICE WATER AND DROWN.
THE ONLY THING THAT COULD POSSIBLY MAKE THIS WORSE WOULD BE IF THE CLASS WAS...
...TAUGHT BY MY SADISTIC BABY SITTER!!
WELL, LOOK WHO'S HERE!
WATERSON

OK... EVERYONE IN THE WATER!
I REFUSE! I'M FREEZING ALREADY!
CALVIN, DO YOU KNOW WHAT A "RAT TAIL" IS?
NO.
IT'S WHEN YOU SOAK A TOWEL AND TWIST IT UP INTO A WHIP. IT STINGS LIKE CRAZY AND IS MUCH WORSE THAN BEING COLD. GET MY DRIFT?
I ALWAYS THOUGHT LIFE-GUARDS WERE JUST TAUGHT HOW TO RESUSCITATE PEOPLE AND THINGS LIKE THAT.
WATERSON

THIS WATER IS FREEZING! I'M GOING TO GO INTO SHOCK AND DROWN, I JUST KNOW IT.
I BET THE LIFEGUARD IS INVOLVED IN SOME INSURANCE SCAM AND SHE'S GOING TO LET US ALL DROWN LIKE RATS! OH NO! OH NO!
OK, FIRST WE'RE GOING TO LEARN THE "DEADMAN'S FLOAT."
MOM!! HELPP! HELPP!
WHAT I PUT UP WITH TO PAY FOR COLLEGE..

I DON'T WANT TO LEARN HOW TO SWIM!
I DON'T NEED TO KNOW HOW. I'LL JUST STAY ON DRY LAND ALL MY LIFE.
WHAT IF YOU FALL OUT OF A BOAT?
NO BIG DEAL.

FORTY MINUTES OF TERROR! WHY DID YOU SIGN ME UP FOR THIS?
WHY NOT SOMETHING FUN, LIKE HANG GLIDING OR SHARPSHOOTING?
...OR DRIVING LESSONS! I COULD BE TAKING DRIVING LESSONS AND LEARNING SOMETHING USEFUL!
HOW ABOUT PIANO LESSONS? YOU START TUESDAY.
ACK! NO NO NO NO NO NO NO NO NO NO NO

HEY, MOM, ARE YOU NERVOUS?
NO. ... WHY?
CALVIN, GO OUTSIDE AND QUIT BUGGING ME!
CALVIN THE BUG BUZZES OFF!
FLYING LOW OVER THE GRASS, HE SEARCHES FOR DEAD MEAT!
UP AND OVER THE FLOWERS, DARTING THIS WAY AND THAT!
OH NO! HE'S CAUGHT IN A SPIDER WEB!
THRASHING ABOUT IN A DESPERATE BID FOR FREEDOM, HE ONLY BECOMES MORE ENTANGLED! SOON THE SPIDER WILL SUCK OUT HIS INNARDS! HELP!
WATERSON
I WAS GOING TO JOIN YOU IN THE HAMMOCK, BUT I THINK I'LL FORGET IT.

HI, CALVIN, WHAT ARE YOU DOING?
BIG IMPORTANT SECRET THINGS! GO AWAY! GET LOST!
ALL RIGHT, DANDELION HEAD! WHO CARES WHAT YOU DO ANYWAY!
*WE'RE* DOING GREAT THINGS. *WE'RE* HAVING **FUN**!
I THOUGHT WE WERE BORED OUT OF OUR SKULLS.
OH HUSH. YOU DON'T KNOW ANYTHING.

THAT STUPID CALVIN. HE'S SO MEAN.
ALL I TRY TO DO IS BE FRIENDS, AND HE TREATS ME LIKE I'M NOBODY.
WELL, WHO NEEDS JERKS LIKE HIM ANYWAY? I DON'T NEED HIM FOR A FRIEND. I CAN HAVE FUN BY MYSELF!
POOP.

SUSIE, HOBBES THOUGHT I WAS RUDE, SO I'M SORRY, AND YOU CAN COME PLAY WITH US IF YOU WANT.
THANKS, CALVIN. THAT'S REALLY NICE OF YOU.
OK, WE'LL PLAY HOUSE NOW. I'LL BE THE HIGH-POWERED EXECUTIVE WIFE, THE TIGER HERE CAN BE MY UNEMPLOYED, HOUSEKEEPING HUSBAND, AND YOU CAN BE OUR BRATTY AND BRAINLESS KID IN A DAY CARE CENTER.
THIS WAS *YOUR* IDEA, PEA BRAIN.
DON'T YOU TALK TO YOUR FATHER THAT WAY!
I'M OFF TO WALL STREET. DON'T WAIT UP.

THE ALIENS ARE GAINING ON OUR HERO! IN A SURPRISE MOVE, SPACEMAN SPIFF SHIFTS INTO REVERSE!
THE ALIENS ROAR AHEAD! SPIFF SHIFTS BACK INTO FORWARD, AND PURSUES THE ALIENS!
...BUT THE ALIENS HAVE TURNED AROUND AND ARE HEADED STRAIGHT FOR OUR HERO! SPIFF SHIFTS INTO REVERSE!
I'M GETTING SICK.

WHACK!
???
TELL ME THIS ISN'T A SPITBALL!!

HOBBES, QUICK! HOW DO I STOP?!?
STEER INTO A GRAVEL DRIVEWAY AND FALL DOWN!
SKRUNCH!
THAT WAS ONLY A SUGGESTION.

BOY, IT'S QUIET AROUND HERE TODAY!
TOO QUIET!
HA HA! GOTCHA!
HEY!
SQUIRT!
SQUIRT!
..RRRRRRRR...
SQUEAK
WHOOSH!
HA HA! GOTCHA BACK!
HEY!
SPLOOSH
A WATER BALLOON! THAT DIRTY TIGER ESCALATED THE WAR! THIS CALLS FOR SUPREME RETALIATION!
I'LL GET HIM WITH THE GARDEN HOSE! NOTHING CAN BEAT A HOSE FOR SHEER VOLUME OF WATER!
...UNLESS, OF COURSE, HE WENT SO FAR AS TO...
WATERSON

LOOK AT THAT THING IN THE DIRT! IT MUST BE A FOSSIL!
I WONDER WHAT PECULIAR ANIMAL **THIS** WAS.
BUT IT'S NOT A BONE. IT MUST BE SOME PRIMITIVE HUNTING WEAPON OR EATING UTENSIL FOR CAVE MEN.
MAYBE IT HAD SOME RELIGIOUS FUNCTION.
THIS EXPLAINS WHY YOUR CLOTHES STAY ON THE FLOOR.

MAKING A SIGN?
I'M DECLARING THE CREEK BACK IN THE WOODS "CALVIN'S CREEK."
WHEN YOU DISCOVER SOMETHING, YOU'RE ALLOWED TO NAME IT AND PUT UP A SIGN.
Calvins CrEEK
BUT SUPPOSE YOU DIDN'T DISCOVER THAT CREEK.
OF COURSE I DID! NOBODY **ELSE** HAS A SIGN THERE, RIGHT?
Hobs Crk

CAN HOBBES AND I GO PLAY IN THE RAIN, MOM?
NO.
WHY NOT?
YOU'LL GET SOAKED.
WHAT'S WRONG WITH THAT?
YOU COULD CATCH PNEUMONIA, RUN UP A TERRIBLE HOSPITAL BILL, LINGER A FEW MONTHS, AND DIE.
I ALWAYS FORGET. IF YOU ASK A MOM, YOU GET A WORST-CASE SCENARIO.
I HAD NO IDEA THESE LITTLE SHOWERS WERE SO **DANGEROUS**.

WANT TO GO SPELUNKING WITH ME?
SPELUNKING? THERE AREN'T ANY CAVES AROUND HERE!
YOU DON'T NEED A CAVE. ALL YOU NEED IS A ROCK.
SPELUNK!
WATTERSON
WELL DAD, OFF TO WORK?
TOO BAD. I'M ON SUMMER VACATION, SO I GET TO STAY HOME AND DO WHATEVER I WANT.
WELL, GO OFF AND JOIN THE RAT RACE! MOM AND I ARE RACKING UP LOTS OF EXPENSES!
OOG.
I JUST DO THAT TO HELP HIM APPRECIATE THE WEEKENDS MORE.
WATTERSON
HOT DAY, ISN'T IT?
I'LL SAY.
BUT IT'S THE HUMIDITY THAT REALLY GETS TO ME.
YOU DON'T LIKE IT WHEN IT'S HUMID?
NOT AT ALL.
THEN YOU'D BETTER GET OUT QUICK.
WATTERSON

GO ON "THREE," OK? ONE..... TWO.....
TWO AND A HALF...
OOMF!
READY.... SET....
GO!
PIT PAT PIT PAT PIT
PAT PIT PAT PIT PAT PI
PITTIDA DITTIDA PITTIDA DITTIDA PITTI
CHOOGA CHOOGA CHOOGA CHOO
EEEE
NYEEOWWW
*GASP* I CAN'T BELIEVE IT! NO SONIC BOOM! NOT EVEN A "POP"!
I HEARD A POP, BUT I THINK IT WAS MY LUNGS.
WATTERSON

WHAT'S FOR DINNER?
SALMON.
SALMON?! BLECCHH!!
CALVIN, ONE OF THESE DAYS YOUR FACE IS GOING TO FREEZE LIKE THAT.
WOW!

HI, HOBBES!
GOOD HEAVENS, WHAT'S WRONG WITH YOU?
MOM SAID IF I KEEP MAKING THIS FACE, IT WILL FREEZE LIKE THIS FOREVER!
YOU REALLY THINK SO?
IT'S WORTH A TRY...
I'LL BET MY FEATURES ARE HARDENING ALREADY.
I ALWAYS LIKED GARGOYLES.

DON'T MAKE FACES AT THE TABLE, CALVIN.
I CAN'T HELP IT.
MOM SAID MY FACE WOULD FREEZE LIKE THIS SOME DAY, AND IT JUST DID.
NO, IT DIDN'T.
IT DID, DAD! MOM WAS RIGHT. I'M HORRIBLY DISFIGURED FOR LIFE.
NO, YOU AREN'T.
BUT DON'T WORRY, I WON'T SPOIL DINNER. SEE? ELEPHANT MAN!

HERE COMES SUSIE.
HA! WON'T SHE BE HORRIFIED TO SEE HOW OUR FACES HAVE TRAGICALLY FROZEN!
HI, SUSIE.
HI, CALVIN.
WHAT DID YOU DO, GET YOUR HEAD STUCK IN THE BLENDER? IT'S AN IMPROVEMENT.

ARE THE COALS HOT?
YES, THEY'RE VERY HOT. I'M JUST ABOUT TO PUT ON THE HAMBURGERS.
BEFORE YOU DO, COULD YOU TOSS IN THE CAN OF LIGHTER FLUID AND MAKE A GIANT FIREBALL?
I'VE GOT THE MOST BORING DAD IN THE WORLD.

WITH THESE SNORKELS, WE CAN STAY UNDER WATER INDEFINITELY.
JUST THINK OF ALL THE FISH WE'LL BE ABLE TO SEE!
WE CAN COLLECT SHELLS!
LET'S GO!
WELL SO FAR, THIS HAS BEEN A MAJOR DISAPPOINTMENT.

YOU KNOW, DAD, IT DISTURBS ME THAT THIS WAGON HAS NO SEAT BELTS AND WOULDN'T SURVIVE A 30 MPH IMPACT WITH A STATIONARY OBJECT.
UM... WHY DO YOU BRING THIS UP?
OH, NO REASON.
WANT TO HELP ME TEST THE THEORY OF RELATIVITY?
SURE.
THE IDEA IS THAT THE FASTER WE GO, THE SLOWER TIME GOES.
GOTCHA. IT'S 10:23.
WHAT TIME IS IT NOW?
10:24. GO FASTER.
WE'RE GOING PRETTY FAST! WHAT TIME IS IT?
10:25. TIME STILL HASN'T STOPPED.
HAS TIME STOPPED **NOW**?
NO, JUST MY HEART.
WELL, IT LOOKS LIKE EINSTEIN'S A FRAUD, WOULDN'T YOU SAY?
NO, HE'S RIGHT! LOOK, MY WATCH ISN'T GOING AT ALL ANY MORE!!

Finis